SO-CNH-218

AUTUMN
RAIN

5/12

DATE DUE

Lamppost Library & Resource Center
Christ United Methodist Church
4488 Poplar Avenue
Memphis, Tennessee 38117

AUTUMN RAIN

growing a
flourishing faith

BILLIE CASH

Billie Cash

Matt 7:6

AMBASSADOR INTERNATIONAL
Greenville, South Carolina • Belfast, Northern Ireland

Autumn Rain:
Growing a Flourishing Faith

© 2004 Billie Cash
All rights reserved
Printed in the United States of America

Cover design & page layout by A & E Media — Paula Shepherd

ISBN 1 932307 33 8

Published by the Ambassador Group

Ambassador Emerald International
427 Wade Hampton Blvd.
Greenville, SC 29609
USA
www. emeraldhouse.com

and

Ambassador Publications Ltd.
Providence House
Ardenlee Street
Belfast BT6 8QJ
Northern Ireland
www. ambassador-productions.com

The colophon is a trademark of Ambassador

I dedicate this book to:

Wayve, Bea, Julia

&

The Memory of
John and June
(Mentors of Flourishing Faith)

&

Robb, Rachel, Hope, Regina
(The Bumper Crop)

"YOU CAN TELL WHAT THEY ARE BY WHAT THEY DO"
Matthew 7:16 (CEV)

Endorsements

"Billie Cash, with her distinctive writing style, touches the listener's heart by giving new life to a tired faith. With her artistry she distinguishes between a newborn faith and one that languishes on the vine. In response to her efforts, the reader understands the message, is thankful for the marching orders, wanting, more than all opportunities this world offers, to respond by stepping out for Jesus Christ. While *Windows of Assurance* tells her life story, and *Light Breaking Through* relates to the awakening of the soul, *Autumn Rain*, with its soft peppering as on a tin roof, fans the spirit of the weary or uncommitted into a mighty flame."

Judy Chatham
Writing Lecturer, Indiana/Purdue University
Indianapolis, Indiana

"With pen in hand, Billie Cash illustrates the impact that Jesus Christ can have in a life.

With the loveliness of misty autumn as her backdrop, she sets the scene as one harvesting an October garden, as step by step she describes the glory that can be ours through agreeing with God about the condition of our life without Him. This book is life changing."

Donna Wilkening
Stonecroft Ministries Regional Administrator
Minneapolis, Minnesota

"*Autumn Rain* beautifully captures the essence of God's promise to nourish faith and strengthen hope in His bountiful harvest of blessings. In this spiritually parched world, it is good to pause and 'drink rain from heaven' daily. Thank you, Billie."

Chris Mills
Richmond Associate, Western Europe
International Mission Board, SBC
Richmond, Virginia

'Billie Cash possesses a unique writing style in which each concise truth presented is like a small fine stitch weaving into a tapestry of God's Truth. What a blessing *Autumn Rain* is! For any precious child of God walking through a present difficulty and wondering why He has permitted these dark threads of sorrow, Billie's poignant sharing of her own 'dark night of the soul' will lift her reader's eyes from focusing upon the painful circumstance to embrace the larger, complete work of the Heavenly Father's unfailing love in their lives."

Antonina Ruth Bruno
Benefits Administrator and Facility Security officer, Technology
Development Associates, Inc.
San Diego California

"Billie Cash's *Autumn Rain* is beautifully and descriptively written—a message of hope, meaning, comfort and transformation through commitment to a loving and faithful Father. Of particular delight to me was the honoring of the life of my beloved Bible teacher whose life has been and continues to be of great impact. I was so blessed by your book."

Florine McKay
Retired businesswoman and philanthropic grandmother
Burr Ridge, Illinois

"Billie…Forever the cheerleader for the Lord and His Wondrous Love…You will be encouraged, challenged and inspired throughout this purposeful journey of faith. This book zooms in on faith like radar. I could not put it down…Will share it in my Bible studies…*Autumn Rain* is profound."

Katheryn H. Mote
Interior Design Consultant
Virginia Beach, Virginia
Naples, Florida

"Autumn Rain brings showers of blessings…in fact a downright deluge. Loved the book…highly recommend it."

JoAnne Boche, ATM
Professional Speaker and Tour Director
Minneapolis. Minnesota

"I am intrigued by your style of writing. Our lives really are like a garden needing the daily care of feeding and watering from the Word of God. This book is true inspiration."

Jane Myre
Mentor to women
Paducah, Kentucky

"Autumn Rain is relevant to the needs of today. It will definitely help you discover how to go through the valleys and mountains of 'unfulfilled longings,' 'disappointments that could be victories,' learning how to live in the in between from 'a to b.' …Billie touches in many ways the 'nerve' of life…the way it is now. You will enjoy reading it for yourself and giving it to someone. Personally it challenged me to move from feeling to freedom! That's a big step."

Millie Dienert
Renowned Bible teacher, Communicator
International Prayer Chairman, BGEA
Blue Bell, Pennsylvania

"If you do not consider yourself a "reader," I suggest you pick up this book and try again!

Billie Cash has a style that is both interesting and stimulating. *Autumn Rain* is packed with timeless truth. It is clear that God has gifted Billie to speak at heart level. Interweaving poetry and prose, she creates a tapestry against which God's love and purpose for our lives is beautifully displayed."

Betty Ruth Barrows Seera
Dayton, Tennessee

"Billie's new book *Autumn Rain* serves as a refreshing reminder that we come into our faith in Christ not just for relationship but also to point others to Him. In the chapter 'Harvest Bounty,' she insightfully writes about the funerals of Johnny and June Carter Cash, making observations on the impact of their faith:

Of Johnny: Heaven and hell battled for him. His wounds were apparent but so was his faith. This was not ambiguous faith but clear-cut Christian faith found in Jesus Christ.

Real faith finds a way to grow.

Of June: Roseanne Cash paid one of the most moving tributes I have ever heard at a funeral—to June, her stepmother. Ironically, it was about not using the word '*step*' in their family for John and June made this distinction when they married. There would be no stepparents and stepchildren. They would be family."

Mark Boorman
Olford Ministries International
Memphis Tennessee

Scripture Page

"The land you are crossing the Jordan to take possession of is a land of mountains and valleys which drinks rain from Heaven...."

"It is a land the Lord your God cares for; the eyes of the Lord your God are continuously on it from beginning of the year to the end...."

"So if you faithfully obey the commands I am giving you today—to love the Lord your God and to serve Him with all your heart and with all your soul, then I will send rain on your land, both autumn and spring rains...."

"...So that you may gather in your grain, new wine and oil...."

"I will provide...and you will eat and be satisfied."

DEUTERONOMY 11:11-15

Acknowledgements

I want to say thank you to my precious praying friends.

You prayed me through once again.

Faithful and true are you, my friends.

The Calder Class was strategic in support once again.

You are a loving and accepting group of people.

Laura Whybrew, Ann Slater, Denise Turner, my mother Frances Hall Blanton, Judy Demaio, Joyce Booker, Pat Maxwell are all my prayer team members.

You are ready to pray when need comes. Thank you.

Peggy Davis, Beth Kelly, Audrey McClung, Peggy McGaha and Hope Roberts continue to pray me through all I do, everywhere. You are the inner circle and I am grateful for your love. Some new folks that God has knitted into my heart in thanksgiving are Donna Wilkining, Lori Affatato and Antonina Bruno. You always respond to prayer needs immediately with such encouragement. My Internet prayer base is tremendous. I need your covering as I write and go. The "prayer alerts" go out and the provision of God comes in for me. Thank you so much.

Special thanks for Peggy Davis's encouragement, my husband Roy's diligence in editing and to my new editor Brent Cook.

God has met me in this book

He will meet you.

I rejoice in women like Wayve Berg Bradley and Bea Bixler who have continued to demonstrate flourishing faith into their eighth decade.

I praise God for missionaries like Frank and Chita Drinkard who live out their faith with tenacity and commitment in another land.

I applaud women like Pam and Judy who have taken God's Love into prison.

He has shown me purpose.

I will never turn back.

I want to love and serve my Lord all the days of my life.

I want to grow flourishing faith.

"Thank you, Lord, for allowing me to write and proclaim Your Love."

Billie Cash

Table Of Contents

I.   PREPARING FOR RAIN—A BEGINNING FAITH

*"The land you are crossing the Jordan to take possession of
is a land of mountains and valleys which drinks rain from
heaven..."* Deuteronomy 11:11

1.   A Promise of Harvest 1
2.   A Beginning Rain 13

Come

II.   SOWING IN SHOWERS—A DEPENDENT FAITH

*"It is a land the Lord your God cares for; the eyes of the Lord
your God are continuously on it from beginning of the year to
the end..."* Deuteronomy 11:12

3.   Planting Truth 29
4.   Watering Hope 41
5.   Discovering Faith 51

Deny

III. SURVIVING THE STORM—A RESPONSIBLE FAITH

*"So if you faithfully obey the commands I am giving you
today—to love the Lord your God and to serve him with all
your heart and with all your soul, then I will send rain on
your land, both autumn and spring rains…"*
Deuteronomy 11:13-14a

6. Strengthening the Root...63
7. Pruning the Vision...73
8. Blooming to Serve 89

Take Up

IV. GATHERING A FRUITFUL HARVEST—A FLOURISHING
FAITH

"…So that you may gather in your grain, new wine and oil…"
Deuteronomy 11:14b

9. Harvest Beauty 115
10. Harvest Blessing...127
11. Harvest Bounty...137

Follow

V. TRANSPLANTING THE SEED—A MENTORING FAITH

"I will provide…and you will eat and be satisfied."
Deuteronomy 11:15

12. Transforming the Landscape 155
13. Bumper Crop Harvest 171

Foreword

God knows what we need. We need Him.

We plant in order to have beauty. He is beauty.

We nurture in order to grow. He is provision.

We must have faith bloom in order to survive. He draws us to His Love.

It is the seed. We receive it.

God's Word promises spring rain. Our growing begins.

But there is MORE.

The autumn rain is the rain of harvest, abundance.

Embracing purpose roots our lives.

Obeying, loving and serving Him grows Beauty.

Reproducing our faith grows the Kingdom of God.

Transforming the landscape is what we were meant to do.

Looking at some mentors who strengthen our faith will cause us to strengthen others.

Cycles of renewal must continue to enrich our faith bloom.

Harvest is coming.

God knows what we need.

The autumn rain will do its work.

Billie Cash

Autumn 2003
Cordova, Tennessee

Preface

My garden whispered today. Change is surely on its way.

It was a comfortable thought, like the vision of a beloved friend coming in the distance to my home. A mixture of reflection, memory and insight swept over me. I must get ready.

A morning breeze brushed my hair with a sigh. A bluejay spied fresh water in the birdbath and then lingered long on the edge. My jasmine waved her graceful arms on the fence and bid adieu to summer.

There was a rustling as the swaying limbs of the pear tree bowed down with relief. Summer is over.

The autumn fern graciously spreading her lacy fan in the humid months will now settle in to embrace the shades of fall.

Verdant foliage will give way to a languishing yellow tinged with a timid brown becoming a burnished gold, allowing rich crimson to creep in, intensifying to a deep claret and finally weathering to a fragile eggplant.

Colors projecting change in life. Change always comes.

The explosive hostas will go to sleep.

The ivy in its unruly fashion will refuse to be ignored and continue to climb the trunk of the maple tree, draping itself down the other side in search of clinging space. Something to hold on to.

My garden is readying itself for autumn, and so must I.

The soil requires intense preparation to energize its soul and is frequently overlooked by the novice full of eager zeal. It is the step of significance. Nutrients completely spent must be fully replenished.

Blooming is exhausting. Plants experience weakness. Stretching towards moisture, searching for sunlight, scavenging what they need from the soil. Depleted now, it is also compacted and must be dug up, tilled, turned over, aerated and yet…

Waiting expectantly are marvelous mums pregnant with buds preparing for birth. Patient pansies are positioning themselves for sunlight. Enduring roses, stoically nonchalant…done for a while, they are planning their comeback.

All will need the autumn rain.

Cycles in our lives are found in the garden.

It has been a blessed year. Grandchildren are growing. Thanksgiving is flowing. Much has gone out. Much needs restoring. Much is required. And so I ponder the change, knowing that I too must be renewed. Harvest is coming.

What is God teaching me? He is causing me to look toward Harvest. What have I planted? He promises that I will reap what I have sown.

Where is my focus? He wants my attention and affection. Whom am I serving? He brings beauty. Will I have abundance? He is training my faith.

"Lord, send the autumn rain."

An unexpected wind swirls in suddenly and plays the wind chimes, sounding notes that echo the coming change.

Music in a minor key. I stand mesmerized with the loveliness of the moment. Lifting my face upward I breathe the smell of rain. The first drops are gentle, refreshing, cool and then they become a movement with the wind.

A steady cadence develops as the rhythm of wind, rain and chiming melody embrace.

The garden drinks deeply and so do I. Showers of promise and praise well up within my heart. We must embrace change.

"Lord of the harvest

Nourish my heart

Water my roots

Grow my trust

Enrich my belief

Prune my motive

Feed my faith

Reproduce your love

Order my harvest."

For I welcome what once I feared. I look for what once I missed. I long for what once I ignored.

I want *Your purpose* to rule, *Your presence* to reign, *Your power* to reveal.

A productive life will finish with flourishing faith.

Send the autumn rain. Harvest time is now.

— Billie Cash

Autumn 2003
Cordova, Tennessee

1

A Promise of Harvest

We have dreams.

Attention…the new cheerleaders for Class of 1961 will be….

Breathlessly I strained to hear the names of each one called out over the school's public address system.

There were ten of them.

I was mentally counting them off and wondering if my name would be on the list.

Seconds passed slowly.

My hands were wrapped inside each other, tense, holding on.

My heart was racing.

My head was ringing with possibility.

At last, I heard my name called out,

…and Billie Hall.

It was the last name, but that did not matter.

I had made it.

Trying to contain my joy, I whispered a prayer. I wanted to run through the building shouting to the world, but I had to walk down a long hall to the principal's office first to make sure that it was true.

What if it were a mistake?

How embarrassing that would be.

As I walked with a trembling heart, I asked God to quiet my thoughts, to center me.

He did.

It was true.

The day had begun as a crisp, dog barking, saddle oxford, September school day in the autumn of 1960. A golden sunlight had raised its banner over us. Schedules had to be sorted and met. Big lumbering yellow school buses manned by drivers we would forever endear ourselves to, arrived carrying students, hanging out of the windows, yelling to their buddies. A slight but noticeable breeze blew in making it an almost pleasant ride.

No rain in sight.

Aboard, guys teased girls and then chased them out the door as soon as the bus stopped, across the driveway into the Gymnasium. Conversations about classes, teachers and the close of summer were on everyone's lips. They had athletic gear in hand, a few books and lots of dreams.

I was one of them.

What would this year bring?

Would it meet my expectations?

What did God have in store for me?

God loves to break into our lives with pleasure.

A harvest rain can come at any moment.

It comes when the soil of your life can receive.

This rain of blessing rolls in and calls forth possibilities we have let go.

But God has not.

A Loving God is always tilling the soil of expectation.

We are interested in triumph.

God is interested in training the victor.

All triumph is the result of training.

This was a dream realized—becoming a cheerleader for the first time in my life as a senior in High School.

Duty and delight, determination, and discipline sprang up within me as the autumn rain fell on a young girl seeking acceptance and belonging.

These promises were about to grow.

God knew when and how.

Moving to Memphis, Tennessee in the tenth grade, I swished into class wearing the feminine flounce and crinoline fashion found in the sleepy southern town of Baton Rouge, Louisiana.

Talk about a transition.

Memphis in 1959 was Preppy country.

All those years of being shuffled from school to school seemed to only showcase my insecurities.

Rejection knocked everywhere.

Words of "You will never be able to...."

I had fantasized capturing the role of cheerleader, being integrated into a group. My chance had come after two years in the same school. This was my thirty-third school to attend.

I was a teacher's nightmare.

Imagine trying to average my grades together.

Dad had gotten a construction job with J. C. Collins and back to Memphis we went.

There was a whisper of permanency blowing in the wind. I knew Memphis better than other places we'd lived. This time we had bought a home on Whiting Road.

A home.

It was located in a new homes area.

There were impatient flowerbeds waiting for activity, fledgling trees, a new fence and neighbors to know.

I was excited about the prospect of this school season.

The senior year is a time of reward built on relationship and effort.

I wanted to experience true friendship.

Fall is the breath of change but also beginnings.

This was the second fall that I was approaching in the same school. I eagerly looked for the new faces each fall in my classes, purposely seeking them out. Then I caught up with the summer's happenings with those I knew from the previous two years.

It was a struggle to adjust to a different school. Students unfamiliar had to feel their way, observing what existed, hoping to fit in there.

I knew how they felt.

Sometimes I met someone who had been there all along. They were just quieter personalities, not a part of the mainstream crowd but no less interesting to me.

I looked for genuineness.

God showed me those who were.

My friend Emily was soft spoken and had the sweetest brown eyes. We worked on science projects together. It was terrific to have someone so patient to help me with such detail. She lived in a spacious home on Park Avenue and I loved to go there.

Emily was genuine.

Jim was unconventional in many ways, talented in music and acting. It was great to work with one so creative.

What promise he had.

In theatre, ability is a benchmark of acceptance.

When word got around that a talent show was in the works, all of the drama students began sorting out what each might do. Jim's band won First place, hands down. I competed by singing the popular piece, "*He.*"

You can imagine what a contrast that was.

Jim actually walked over to me and, with sensitivity in his voice, said, "You know what, you shoulda won, cause you can sing but the crowd is the crowd. They wanted rhythm and noise and we gave it to them."

Just hearing his assessment of my performance bolstered my desire to keep on keeping on.

Words of affirmation are gifts.

God arranges those.

He promises a harvest.

Then there was Eva who was in my typing class. Our eyes would meet with the same look when our eccentric teacher said something funny. We both had difficulty with typing tests. My brain and my hand would not cooperate together in speed.

I could not type fast.

Once I was so rattled, I actually spelled an inappropriate word over and over again by mistake because of the proximity of the letters found on the keyboard.

One was an "a" and the other was an "s".

I was horrified and could not turn my paper in after the test. Eva and I joked later about it. She felt the same aloneness that I did at times in class, the isolation of not belonging. Eva possessed a great warm heart and thirty years later God would reconnect us.

I made friends with the ordinary people in my school.

After all I was one of them.

I loved reaching out.

I needed what I gave—encouragement.

I really was a cheerleader.

So at the end of my junior year, when tryouts were scheduled, I decided to go for it.

I learned that I would have to prepare to execute three cheers and perform them on stage for the entire student body. Thank goodness no gymnastics were required in this decade, just enthusiasm, spirit and some ability to project. Most cheerleading experiences begin in Junior High and just gather momentum through out High School.

No one just decides as a senior to try for a cheerleading position

No one but me.

I had the summer to train for this opportunity.

Indeed it seemed mostly a popularity thing. I suspected that my attempt might be hopeless. Still considered a newcomer of only two years, I longed to belong. Comfortable on stage, the speech department became my home.

Laughter was my gift. I could make people laugh, tearing down ridicule while building confidence and polishing my communication skills at the same time.

I studied others and consciously strove to integrate change.

One thing had to go—the way I dressed.

Fashion tends to isolate or include.

I knew which category I was in and what I must do.

Less is better.

In subtle ways, I toned my choices down until they gradually slipped into a tailored look.

A formula evolved.

Look in the mirror and take something off.

That's what I did.

Cluttered and overdone became classic.

It worked.

Now I needed a cheering plan.

I would purpose to practice diligently every day, try to improve form, generate energy and create momentum.

I imagined success.

I envisioned winning but I would leave the outcome in God's Hands.

I prayed.

All kids send arrow prayers. You shoot them at God and hope He gets it.

"Help me, Lord. I hope you will."

Mine were more than arrows. I believed in prayer because my relationship to God was my surest treasure.

Long ago as a child searching, I had discovered the love of Jesus and my need for His Love brought me to belief.

He became my Lord and Savior.

He listened when I prayed and carried my hurts.

He had my heart.

I trusted Him.

The day the votes were cast and counted, I know He encouraged people to vote for me because it was the ordinary people who opened this door.

I knew He had.

I was the only cheerleader who was not a member of a sorority.

I had to have friends from all the various groups in order to win because I had no group. I had no label.

This was not elation I experienced. It was breakthrough.

God did it.

They did not know He did, but I did.

That late September afternoon with the touch of fall in the air was a beginning for me. After the giggles, excitement, and surprise rushed over me, I realized that I had missed my school bus and would have to take a city bus to get home. As I figured out which corner on Poplar Ave I would have to walk to, I felt the first sprinkle of the autumn rain. Gray clouds had been gathering outside the school window while I was celebrating in my soul, thanking God for this unbelievable victory.

Oblivious to the weather, I now had to walk about four blocks to the corner of Poplar and Mendenhall to catch the late afternoon bus. As I headed that way, the rain began to pelt me, gradually soaking me through and through as I finally arrived at the stop.

Waiting in the rain.

There was no bus shelter in those days and I had no umbrella but it didn't matter.

I began to review with spiritual eyes God's faithfulness to me.

I associated all success with Him.

Tears of gratitude spilled over and ran down my cheeks but since I was standing in rain, it didn't matter.

He sent the autumn rain that day to me, washing away my anxiety, encouraging me to believe more, pressing me to trust His vision, His plans.

As a cheerleader I would learn to cheer my football team on in any weather because I was committed, even in driving rain.

A pattern was emerging.

Seek, trust and obey.

When you do, you can expect.

The soil of my life was being plowed. I needed a faith that would produce good fruit.

I did not understand then what I do now.

God wants each of us to have a life of faith that will continue to grow.

"For we are to be...more than conquerors." (Note 1)

"I shall never be like that, we feel. They won...step by step; by little acts of will. Little denials of self, little inward victories, by faithfulness in very little things, they become what they are. No one sees these little hidden steps, they only see the accomplishment...there is no sudden triumph, no spiritual maturity that is not the work of a moment." (Note 2)

God knows every little step we take because when we belong to Him, He prepares those tiny steps.

He has dreams far greater than ours.

His are infinite.

"...This land you are crossing the Jordan to take possession of is a land of mountains and valleys that drinks rain from heaven." **Deuteronomy 11: 11**

What a description of our lives!

Mountains and valleys.

God tills our soil with experience and reveals He was there all the time.

He knows when to send the rain and we must have it.

We cannot BECOME if we do not COME.

"If any one would COME after me...." (Note 3)

Not every one comes.

BUT

He calls us.

He's calling you.

We either run toward God or run away from Him.

He knows the pitfalls along the way.

Our trophies have to be laid down if we COME.

"He who trusts in himself is a fool." (Note 4)

A reigning God knows when to send the Harvest Rain.

Real life is an inside job.

God knows the heart.

Sin compacts the heart and it must be plowed up.

It is the ugliness in our lives that keeps us from God.

Faith must have a beginning.

It does when we acknowledge we need God because of sin.

"Then I acknowledged my sin to you.... I said, 'I will confess...and you forgave.'" (Note 5)

Seek, trust and obey.

Choice shapes our lives.

Victories are short lived.

Learning to be a victor is a forever training.

We ask ourselves questions.

We will have disappointment but can God use it?

We will have setbacks but is God in them?

We will have change, but is God urging a new direction?

We will overcome if God is in our midst because He orchestrates all that concerns us.

Yes, yes, YES, if we COME.

I thought my desire to be a cheerleader and the achievement of it was just a reward of the moment, a teenager's dream.

I was planning to work at being effective.

I was to learn much more.

God was showing me principles about living in this world.

I would get better as my skill increased but spiritually my heart had to be constantly open to Him.

He was establishing my identity.

"In him we live and move and have our being" (Note 6)

Equipping to do the task ahead would always come after my heart was enlarged.

"Enlarge the place of my tent...do not hold back...lengthen your chords, strengthen your stakes." (Note 7)

I must seek, trust and obey.

I must live from a heart that would anticipate God.

He would show me what was there each day.

He would plow it with His Truth.

The soil would need constant replenishment.

Rain would come.

A caring God would send it if I would obey.

Today I am still a cheerleader and still learning.

" But encourage one another as long as it is called Today, so that none of you may be hardened by sin...." (Note 8)

Somewhere in this world, every day, someone needs a beginning.

Do you?

If you do, I am here to cheer you on.

Begin with Jesus.

God has a beginning planned with you in mind.

Seek, trust and obey.

PONDER POINT:

- What is keeping you from relationship with God?
- Was there an experience that you now recognize as God's training for your life's purpose?
- Have you now recognized your need for God?
- Will you COME and begin with HIM?

PRAYER POINT:

"Father,

How awesome is the possibility that we can begin with YOU today.

How suddenly clear it has become that we have been on a journey toward YOU all along but did not realize it until today.

Purpose has eluded us because we have not known Your Presence.

The mountains have crushed us,

The valleys have swallowed our dreams.

We have feared rain.

YOU were watching.

Come now into my expectation, Lord Jesus, through the CROSS.

It rained that day on Calvary when you died for my sin. It was your blood paying for all my self-effort, my struggle to be loved unconditionally.

Sin I carried and sin you covered.

I want my faith to begin.

Come into my life.

Thank you for the care that is now mine forever as a child of God.

Lay the foundation of faith with the soil of your love.

I receive and I believe.

In Jesus' Name, I now have the beginning that matters.

2

A Beginning Rain

God has plans.

Every principle we need is modeled in God's Word.

He has allowed us to meet people who were tasked by Him with bigger-than-life challenges.

Their stories stretch our imagination causing us to observe and wonder how they did what they were asked to do.

God has done this on purpose.

Why?

They help us find ours.

There was a man named Noah.

Who was he?

"He was a righteous man, blameless among the people of his time, and he walked with God." (Note 1)

What was the world like back then?

"...*It was corrupt and full of violence*" (Note 2)

What do we know about the people of this time?

"...*All the people on earth had corrupted their ways.*" (Note 3)

God was choosing a man to mirror obedience to a faithless, dissolute people living in a coercive immoderate society.

Sounds like today.

Enter Noah.

Did he think out loud when he heard the dimensions of the "thing" he was to build?

I would have.

The size alone defies comprehension.

It was mammoth; 450 feet long, 75 feet wide and 45 feet high. (Note 4)

Noah did not know what an ark was, but he followed the instructions given.

There is no mention of him having visualized such an undertaking.

According to scripture there is no evidence of questioning, debating or even procrastinating. Noah just obeyed God.

Not so with us.

Noah walked with God.

That's it.

Noah had relationship.

Trust precedes obedience.

If we can trust God, we can do the incredible.

Reminds me of the truth found in an old hymn, "*When you walk with the Lord in the Light of His word...trust and obey for there's no other way.*"

In this case there was no other way.

God made a covenant with him, an agreement that was binding.

God keeps His Word.

Noah trusted God.

The earth was to be destroyed by a flood, whatever a flood was.

No one had ever seen rain.

There was no preconceived concept about a flood or ark building.

Noah obeyed God.

Two by two of every living creature were to be allowed to go into the ark, plus enough food supplies were stored for all the animals and for Noah's family as well.

How did he know how much food to bring?

Would we?

Obedience opens the way to insight.

"Noah did everything just as God commanded him." (Note 5)

Having never seen rain, he built for the phenomenon of rain.

Not knowing what God was doing with him, he responded.

At the completion of his task, into the ark he went, entourage and all.

God closed the door.

Noah believed God.

Obedience is not an option when a man walks with God.

The project took one hundred and twenty years to complete.

Now, that does not compute with our present day understanding but remember he was 500 years old when he fathered his sons. (Note 6)

God Almighty sets times and boundaries for every generation.

"...He *determined* the times set for them and the exact places where they should live." (Note 7)

Remember this is a beginning for Noah.

God likes to cause new things to happen.

By faith Noah entered into relationship with the eternal God.

By faith we receive God's Word as true.

> "To strive with difficulties, and to conquer them is the highest human felicity." —**Samuel Johnson**

Will we be asked to do difficult things?

We will.

Does God know the degree of difficulty?

He does.

Will we act in faith upon the unknown because we believe God will guide us?

Noah did.

Did he pick up a saw and a hammer and begin?

Did he assemble his materials as he went along?

Did sit down and think about the scale of this project?

Did count the cost in humiliation?

What did his family think?

Were they supportive?

Were they helpers in this?

We do not know the answers but we do know God made a way for Noah.

Faith stretches our reason.

What was it like to hear the sound of rain for first time, to see moisture form in the window of the ark, the only window to the world?

It must have been puzzling.

Perhaps it was a gentle tapping at first followed by a steady beat, continuing for days upon days until Noah wondered if it would ever stop.

Distracting him from other duties.

There was a lot going on in the ark.

Animals and families need a lot of tending.

And yet inside, he and his family were safe.

This boat began to maneuver.

It must have been unsettling to sense the movement of the monstrous ark rising beneath them with buoyancy, carrying people, supplies and animals safely as his scoffers were now silenced.

Their words rang in his head.

No one believed him.

They all perished.

Their ridicule seemed brittle now.

Perhaps a time or two, they had come close to breaking his focus, but the provision of God intervened.

He was there all the time.

And Noah kept going.

Obedience obliterated the obstacles and made way for anticipation.

Did doubt ever try to defeat?

Was discouragement looming over him daily?

Did he know God would not fail?

There is no journal of his thoughts, only a record of his action.

Here is what he did:

Noah built something unknown—an ark.

Prepared to experience a supernatural unknown—rain.

Because of the KNOWN—God.

He knew God—The Great I Am.

All of his life had prepared him to be able to do this work.

God called Noah.

God is faithful.

God calls you and me.

The ark found land at last and God gave a promise never again to flood the earth.

He sealed his love for Noah with a rainbow.

Every time we see one, we are reminded of the faithfulness and creativity of God.

Our life experiences prepare us to be ready, to hear the call of God, to obey.

God trains through experience.

Remembering His provision helps us continue.

Drawing us to another level of trust, He expects us to exercise our faith.

We must when we have new beginnings.

I recall a precarious musical debut that occurred when Kellye was in the ninth grade.

By then music had become an important influence in her life.

Piano lessons began at age nine and by age fourteen she began to perform.

There came an opportunity to play the piano in a school talent show.

It was the first time she had competed.

Beginnings are important.

Excited and expectant, her best friend Sonja was also going to play the piano in the event.

They both took lessons from the same teacher and were close friends.

Practicing religiously, they both talked about each respective piece, looking forward to the show.

The evening arrived.

Kellye was playing the flamboyant, Spanish selection, *"Maleguena."*

She was slated in the program to perform before her friend Sonja was to play.

Sitting down and positioning herself before the imposing, shining black grand piano, she adjusted the bench, touched the keyboard with a precise but charismatic touch and began.

I could see giftedness begin to unfold.

The ability to captivate an audience, inviting them into the music is what every young talent hopes to do.

Kellye had presence.

She was prepared to give her best.

Within moments, a problem became blatantly obvious.

The technician had forgotten to secure the piano's rolling legs with blocks!

With each note that her fingers played, there was a magnetic loveliness in the music and yet another diversion was developing before the eye of the audience.

The piano was actually moving away from her.

She did not know what was happening.

Concentrating more and playing this rhythmic, colorful piece with great flare, she became more determined to continue, trying to hold on to the performance. Her hands would fly across the keyboard earnestly reaching for the keys while the piano was unrelentingly moving away from her.

Straining forward she would not quit.

We sensed her frustration.

But also her resolve to finish what she had begun.

When the last measure was played with only the tips of her fingers, she stood up and bowed to the audience in exasperation as they gave her roaring applause.

The dilemma had been revealed completely and was remedied immediately for her friend Sonja.

There would not be a runaway piano this time.

As a result, Sonja's performance was technically flawless.

The instrument, now stationary, would not escape as it had for

Kellye.

Sonja won the competition that evening.

Kellye ran to congratulate her and then ran weeping to the car.

I was so proud of her.

Mom the cheerleader began to tell her how fantastic it was to see a performer so concentrated, so able, pouring her music out through her fingertips in spite of a piano that refused to be still.

Sonja captured the trophy.

Kellye captured the audience.

There is…"The harvest of a quiet eye." **—William Wordsworth**

I had been watching, observing intently and praying, keenly aware of all that surrounded her.

It was a moving experience that moved her to another plateau of confidence.

One we would never forget.

Kellye was being equipped.

God was watching.

She had executed with her whole heart.

The unexpected happened.

She did not panic or fold.

She purposed to finish, to hold on.

The soil of her life was being dug up and readied.

Calamity could not break her concentration.

Pressure is neutralized by preparation.

Life does have mountains and valleys.

That night was a valley.

Kellye had in place a relationship to her Lord and Savior.

She knew He was there.

God was going to use music as a discipline in the blossoming of her faith.

He uses everything in our lives.

When we begin with God he becomes the author of our beginnings.

In the Old Testament there was a king named Uzziah. At the age of sixteen he ascended to the throne. Everything he attempted to do was successful. He literally rebuilt his land, taking the city of Elath in southern Judah, expanding the armies.

He even *"...dug many cisterns, because he had much live stock in the foothills and plains. He had people working in his fields and vineyards...for he loved the soil."* (Note 8)

He succeeded because *"God helped him."* (Note 9)

"As long as the heart of Uzziah humbly sought the Lord, God prospered him." (Note 10)

Seeking after God is the key,
Humbly.

Uzziah had the good fortune to have the prophet Zechariah to cheer him on in his pursuits. Under his divine guidance, the fledgling king continued to succeed for a time.

Pride ferociously pursued him and eventually found a way to enter his heart.

Too soon he forgot where the blessing originated.

Blessing is from God.
He looks for people who walk with Him.

Kellye was about to experience a harvest blessing.

In September of 1986, she approached center stage in Atlantic City's Boardwalk Hall to perform before 30,000 people.

Once again a formidable black grand piano dominated the stage.

She would be singing and playing the Vicki Carr rendition, *"I'll Be Home."*

With authority and grace, clarity and power, she moved the audience to the edge of their seats.

This time the piano did not move.

Our hearts did.

When she was finished, we were standing and she was receiving deafening applause, flowing with favor and a Heavenly Father was cherishing all.

He knew it would come.

Momentous blessing rained down upon Kellye as He gave her the reign of Miss America.

Long ago the soil of her heart had been tilled and trained for such a time as this.

God called her to be His and then gave her a work to do.

She persevered.

She learned there would be days of sacrifice.

She became a seeker.

Principles evolved.

Train.

Finish what you start.

Don't lose focus.

Believe.

Anticipate God.

Trust and obey.

It all begins with relationship.

God calls us.

He says, "COME."

God called Noah. Noah obeyed God.

He followed through with expectancy.

God called Kellye. Kellye worked the plan He gave.

Both had to listen to God's voice and He used many people along the way to encourage.

Both had to leave their comfort zone.

Both were not perfect.

Neither are we.

Noah messed up once he got to dry land.

But what happened to Noah then did not negate what God had accomplished through him.

Sin is ugly and moves us to the precipice of pride.

We must move back to center where a Sovereign Lord dwells who forgives and restores.

He does so through our heart.

We all mess up.

God is in every pressure, every time line, every detail in the life of a believer.

He still is.

He wants to move us to COME to Him.

What a Savior we have.

What a future He has for us.

After all, He is God…and we are not.

"A life devoted to riches is a dead life, a stump.
A God shaped life is a flourishing tree." (Note 11)

"Happiness is simply growth…we are happy when we are growing." **—William Butler Yeats**

And flourishing trees must have rain.

God knows what we need.

He begins with the heart.

It is where we must begin.

Harvest is always on God's mind.

He will bring the rain.

> "The sun does not shine for a few trees and flowers, but for the wide world's joy." —**Henry Ward Beecher**

And with joy, the Son of God pursues us, to bless us, to grow us.

He wants our lives to be a garden of beauty.

Today He says, "COME."

PONDER POINT:

- Can I look back and see how the Hand of God was training me?
- Am I willing to obey and follow through when I cannot comprehend His plan?
- What are the requirements for blessing?
- Will I act upon what I know and hang on?

PRAYER POINT:

Father,

Your banner over us is Love.

When I am plodding along with no evidence of success,

When I am weary of continuing,

When I do not anticipate the coming rain that I desperately need, I will choose to remember this; You are there.

Keep me. Hold me. Guide me.

I will believe by obeying and completing what you charge me to do.

Some days it will be pure joy.

You will be smiling over me.

Some days I will want to run away.

You will be disciplining me.

Some days I will mess up.

You will forgive and redirect me.

I cannot lose with YOU.

I will love YOU more each day.

I will trust Your Timing.

Forgive my proud and self-orchestrating ways.

Father, I Come.

Lamppost Library & Resource Center
Christ United Methodist Church
4488 Poplar Avenue
Memphis, Tennessee 38117

Come

With bowed heads and open hearts may we offer ourselves,
We can do no more, and we dare do no less.
B. F. Wescott

Planting Truth

Truth must begin.

We all live by some standard.

If I lift weights I will get results.

Building muscle requires an intelligent knowledge of the body and a will to execute a plan.

Small weights must be used first to condition the muscles.

When repetitions become too easy more weight must be added to increase strength.

If I keep at the program I will not only experience a toned body but also I will have stronger bones and more energy, added benefits.

Eating nutritious food will require some effort.

Getting enough rest will balance out the equation.

A resilient, healthy life needs all of this.

I make a decision with my will.

Set backs will come.

If I try this for a season and quit, I will notice the change.

Muscle mass will diminish.

Becoming weaker physically, my body will retreat.

If I return to what I know works, again I will see results and move forward.

Forward or Backward.

Choice.

Whose?

Yours and mine.

That's the human condition of our faith journey as well.

Seasons of strength and joy because of discipline

OR

Seasons of sloth and jeopardy because of delay.

It has always fascinated me that Bible stories tell it all, the good, bad and the ugly.

When people do the right thing, there is precious blessing;

When they do the wrong thing, there is painful consequence.

Knowledge of the Word of God builds our lives from the inside out because it is Truth.

We are supposed to live from a heart grounded in Truth and in tune with God through relationship.

"Many things are trying to play upon the beautiful instrument of the heart. The devil is a master at manipulating the heart. How will you know what is compelling you?" (Note 1)

"Who can map out the various forces at play in one soul?" asked Augustine, a man who was the first to write out the story of listening to his heart. "Man is a great depth, O Lord...but the hairs of his head are easier by far to count than...the movements of his heart." (Note 2)

David's story is given to us in God's Word for just such an examination.

He was an unlikely candidate for king.

Samuel was summoned to find and anoint a king from among the seven sons found in the line of Jesse.

One by one they filed by and were rejected.

"So he asked Jesse, are these all the sons you have? There is still the youngest…but he is tending sheep." (Note 3)

And so David was sent for and the Lord instructed Samuel to anoint him.

The runt, the least impressive and credentialed.

BUT

David, being a shepherd was fit physically because herding sheep is a robust job of manual labor.

Sheep are always wandering.

They need a shepherd.

He had figured out how to live. Scripture describes David as *"ruddy, with a fine appearance and handsome features."* (Note 4)

I imagine that nights lived out in the field with no one to deal with but his sheep could have given David some great moments of beauty under the stars as he played his music and learned to depend upon God.

His love for God grew and his heart changed because David knew his God returned the love.

God leads the way in truth because He is Truth.

"Teach me your way Oh Lord and I will walk in your truth.
Give me an undivided heart…." (Note 5)

David was being trained from the heart to become a king after God's heart.

The Bible is filled with the adventures of David as king.

Triumphs on the battlefields,

Favor with the people.

We looked inside an unlikely friendship that God put together between David and Jonathan, Saul's son.

We saw envy and jealousy from King Saul as his tormented life would reach for David's music and be soothed and then push him away when ambition was threatened.

David faced extremes.

And yet, as long as his heart was not divided, he overcame the turmoil.

Music was the balm to his soul in times of isolation, confusion and angst.

A heart opened to the melodies of heaven sang of the truths that sustained him.

Strengthened himself, he was able to calm the depressed Saul's anxiety.

God had watered the seed of truth in David's life through many seasons in shepherd life.

Why?

Truth was planted in his heart.

David had heart health.

David—the mighty warrior, virile, persuasive, always pursuing God's heart—was spiritually fit.

Until we get to II Samuel Chapter 11.

Out of step with God.

In step with disaster

David took a break.

And we suddenly see ourselves.

We take breaks, don't we?

A break from truth.

One day won't matter.

One prayerless day

One piece of forbidden fruit

One secret moment.

But it does.

We discover that David wasn't where he was expected to be.

*"In the spring at the time when kings go off to war, David sent Joab out with the king's men and the whole Israelite army. They destroyed the Ammonites and besieged Rabbah. But **David remained in Jerusalem.**"* (Note 6)

What happens to us when we take a break from truth?

We lose integrity.

Our hearts become divided.

That's what happened to David.

Does God know our areas of weakness?

Does He care about us?

Does He watch over our lives?

"...It is a land the Lord your God cares for; the eyes of the Lord are continuously upon it from the beginning of the year to the end." **Deuteronomy 11: 12**

He knew where David was.

He knows where we are.

Because David was not where he was supposed to be, his bored and wandering eyes fell upon a beautiful woman named Bathsheba, bathing on the rooftop of the house next door.

What harm is there in looking?

Just a casual look at another woman.

She was married.

He desired her.

Casual was now a course headed towards calamity.

An inquiry brought truth.

He ignored it.

She conceived.

There was a fork in the road, a place of hesitation.

There always is.

David got caught up in expediency, an adrenaline rush.

He stepped over into forbidden territory.

His heart was compromised.

Consequence was ahead.

A cover up was ordered.

The husband, Uriah the Hittite, was now summoned home, encouraged to spend the night with his wife in the vain hope that this untimely pregnancy might be concealed.

Covering your sin never works.

Uriah had more integrity than his king.

He knew his men could not come home and be with their families so he felt he should not do so either.

Instead, Uriah *"slept at the entrance to the palace with his master's servants and did not go down to his house."* (Note 6)

Integrity again.

David's scheme did not work but he could not stop.

Deliberately getting Uriah drunk, he hoped Uriah would finally go home, spend the night with his wife and the rest would be history.

He would not.

Stage two of cover up.

Joab, his replacement, was ordered to send Uriah to the front lines where the fiercest fighting would be.

In this act, Uriah met his death.

The news came back to his widow who dressed in mourning.

After the time of mourning was over, she came into David's house, became his wife and bore the child, a son.

For an instant the grave injustice looked as though it would go undetected.

But God had been watching.

He misses nothing.

No small discrepancy or blatant blunder can hide from the Sovereign Lord.

He is Truth.

"...The thing David had done displeased God." (Note 8)

Each time we take a break from truth, God is displeased with us.

He has a standard.

It is given to us in His Word that we might hide it in our hearts and not sin.

His ways are pure and undefiled.

He looks at the heart

Truth will always expose the lie, the false.

A loving God purposed that a man named Nathan be sent to David.

Revelation comes to the believer.

Nathan relates to David a story that will bring forth truth.

A rich man had many cattle and sheep.

A poor man only had one little ewe lamb

A traveler passing by needed a meal.

The rich man hoarded his livestock and took this little ewe lamb belonging to the poor man, preparing it for the traveler's meal.

Upon hearing this story, David, outraged, demanded this rich man pay for the lamb four times over and then pay with his life.

This was the moment of Truth.

Nathan said, *"You are the man."* (Note 9)

The arrow of reality pierced David's heart.

Why?

Because truth was planted there long ago.

A scathing indictment followed.

Accused of despising the Word of God by doing what is evil in God's sight,

The mighty king was brought to repentance.

Repentance, the gift of Godly sorrow over sin.

We know what we have done.

We are accountable for our actions.

We can turn back to Truth.

The God who watches over us from the beginning of the year to the end is vigilant.

David, who took a break from truth, who was not where he should have been, who could have chosen not to commit adultery, who caused a man to be murdered, this David declared, *"I have sinned against God."* (Note 10)

Showers of remorse;

Reaping and sowing are a part of the law of the harvest.

"You can't sow disrespect, hatred…dishonesty and expect to reap honor, love, wisdom truth." (Note 11)

His sin was forgiven.

The child's life was the price.

There is always cost when we move away from truth.

And yet the ever-vigilant God who knows all, continuously watching over us, reaches down, blessing the union of David and Bathsheba with the birth of Solomon and the scripture says, *The Lord loved him.* (Note 12)

Premeditated crime by one who knew better.

Forgiven,

Renewed.

Blessed again.

That is the God of Truth.

Planting truth in your heart's garden is wise.

When devastation comes and rips your life into shreds, if truth has been planted, it will spring up, revitalized, reminding you of who you are.

A restored life because of Truth,

A heart reclaimed through repentance.

A body refreshed, gloriously vigorous and healthy once again.

Truth heals.

We have parents who have not modeled right and wrong before their children.

Accountability has not been taught.

We have seen the cycle of brokenness; scandal, promiscuity and disease overtake our homes.

We have refused to acknowledge our sin.

We blame others.

We take a break from truth and when we do, our spiritual muscles sag and our joy is depleted.

The light we carried with pride is quenched.

Our effectiveness is compromised.

A loving God in mercy sends someone along to come after us with Truth, pursuing until we turn around, repent and embrace the standard once again found in God's Word.

"I will give them an undivided heart and put a new spirit in them...." (Note 13)

God's Spirit in us quickens when we are called back to Truth and once again we are undivided.

He watches and waits;

Forward or Backward.

He's there.

And then we become the cheerleaders, cheering others because we have been broken by choice.

So pick up a weight and start over.

Get a plan.

Act on the piece of truth you know.

Flex your will and get it in line with His.

Get fit for the Kingdom.

Expect God to be watching.

Watching and watering the seed of our lives with showers of blessing.

He is Truth.

Harvest is on His mind,

And so are you.

PONDER POINT:

- Why is knowledge of God's Word necessary for truth to be planted in your life?
- Why do you resist the daily discipline of right living?
- Have you taken a spiritual break?

PRAYER POINT:

Father;

We all have walked away from truth at some time or another.

Forgive our sin.

Lord, to know the way to live in YOU and to become lazy is childish, shallow.

To lose our focus and wander into a place YOU never intended is deception.

And yet we have done so.

To repent and be forgiven is life given back, Hallelujah!

Oh to taste the joy of forgiveness—to know we have been redeemed and can start over. What a God we have!

One who watches over us continuously.

That is the God of Truth.

Help us to plant truth in our heart each day and to care for it and protect it.

Thank YOU that you hear when we call and that YOU are waiting to bring us back. Establish our way in truth and we shall recognize it when we see it.

Oh, Love that will not let go of me;

I praise YOU and bow down before Your Truth.

4

Watering Hope

Love brings hope.

Plants need watering.
So does faith.

Last fall we decided to extend the front flowerbed so that it would cascade to the street. There was a lot of work to be done and some concerted thought put into the design of the plantings.

Since the original area is terraced, we chose to continue the unruly trail of the English Ivy already in place in the upper section. It needed training to move down the bank, creating a ground cover that would hold the soil, protecting it from erosion.

Functional but attractive was our goal.

Hostas were chosen because they are an ever-present comeback each year.

They wake up in the spring and take charge in the summer.

In the fall they start to go to sleep, becoming dormant through the winter.

The importance of getting them into the soil and watered adequately is what begins to establish them.

I chose hostas because they are dependable and a perfect backdrop for the spring and summer flowering plants, adding color from season to season.

They literally explode in the spring.

You wake up one morning, go into the garden and overnight they have emerged.

Leafy variegated green fans shoot up and unfurl, shouting their arrival.

You can count on them every year.

To get them firmly imbedded, a systematic and thorough watering must occur.

The drought in a southern summer can cause foliage to collapse; but with a timely shower, lush, verdant leaves will appear.

Even though they are winding down in the fall, they still need moisture to store up what is required to get through the cocoon of winter.

God's showers have minerals that ordinary water does not have.

He knows when plants need water.

He knows when our souls are dry and faith is fainting.

How does He know?

"…The Lord your God cares…." Deuteronomy 11:12a

He cares about mountains, valleys, land, gardens, your life and mine.

Life is in the rain for the plant.

Timing the showers is a strategy of His.

He knows when to birth hope.

Yesterday while I was looking over some old tapes and doing some sorting, I came upon the song *"Total Praise"* recorded by Brooklyn Tabernacle choir. It is a stirring piece of music that moves across the heart with such spiritual power that one is compelled to enter into praise and thanksgiving, for the presence of God is released.

It is more.

It is awe.

And so I did.

Praise to the One true God.

Words that bring Hope welled up within me.

"You are the source of my strength. You are the strength of my source...I lift my hands in total praise to you...."

I listened, worshiped, wept and remembered a time several years ago, when the Thompson family, who had lost a beloved son to cancer, sang it.

It became an offering, a sacrifice representing their assurance about Robert their son.

Assurance born of Hope.

A young wife and four sons were left behind.

Never have I witnessed such an integrated depth of God's abiding love in a family.

A crisis of faith.

Theirs was unshakable.

"I have set the Lord always before me.
Because he is at my right hand,
I will not be shaken." (Note 1)

Showers had come to water the seed of belief planted long ago in One greater, and Hope was birthed.

Today I called R.E., the father and once again he reiterated the faithfulness of God to his daughter-in-law, Jennifer and four growing grandsons.

And God showered my faith and hope grew.

When we hope we grow.

We find God watering hope in ordinary places as well.

His name was Jeff.

He worked as a cook in a Japanese restaurant here in Memphis.

It had been a disappointing day for me.

I had driven with my mother Frances to my first book signing for my first book, *Windows of Assurance* in a small town about ninety minutes away.

The day had been a dismal failure for me and for the owner of this small bookstore.

We both had high hopes.

Rainy weather could have brought people into the bookstore but did not.

The intermittent showers seemed to keep folks at home.

It was a sleepy Saturday.

One friend had come.

When it became apparent that she was the only one to come to the bookstore, we made light conversation, ate a bite of lunch, swallowing our pride, and after two hours left, feeling dejected.

Hopeful had become less.

Driving back to Memphis in the showers I decided to treat Mother to a dining experience as a way to end our discouraging dilemma.

She had never been to a restaurant where the food is prepared at the table over a large stainless steel grill by a skillfully trained and highly entertaining chef.

The art of Japanese cooking is pure drama, producing a delectable cuisine delivered with fun and flair.

Enter Jeff.

He came to our table bringing his tray of well-cared-for cooking instruments.

He needed all of them.

With a twinkle in his eye, he welcomed us, proceeding to take our order.

On our right was a family consisting of what appeared to be a mother,

father, two small middle school children and a doting grandmother. Later that was confirmed. They were pleasant and absorbed in their own conversation.

On our left was an attractive blonde lady, about thirty, who was busy chatting very animatedly with a young girl who looked about ten years old. Later on my mother discovered that this lady was a teacher who had planned this meal as a special treat for her student who was competing in gymnastics.

I made an interesting observation as I sat down and our meal began.

It is impossible to remain compartmentalized in this setting.

People are sitting around the grill like one big family.

Eventually one must interact in some way with another as the meal progresses.

The chef sets the stage.

Knives are whisked into the air and land precisely in his hand on cue and sometimes in his hat.

Eggs are thrown and spiral in such a way that they fall gently onto his oversized spatula and are only broken at will in an exact moment he chooses.

Fire sweeps across the grill unexpectedly and flames reach up for a crescendo to punctuate the performance and start the juices flowing to hunger.

It works.

Pure entertainment at its best.

We were laughing and ready to eat.

There was Another orchestrating this evening.

God had brought this group together.

A fragile faith was about to get a shot of hope.

Jeff was a tall, slender Asian fellow in his twenties.

His smile was engaging, his manner friendly.

He began his food preparation, laying out the vegetables, dousing them with lemon, water and herbs.

A couple of times I thought we would be wearing some of the ingredients but he always managed to catch them just in time.

An artistic juggler.

At one point he asked me a question I did not expect.

With direct eye contact he said, "And what do you do?"

Now no one else had been asked that question.

Only me.

I was startled.

This man who did not know me, had never seen me, was cooking dinner for me had asked me what I do.

Presumptuous, I'm thinking.

But in an instant I sensed more than what was asked.

God was cooking up something else along with my food.

Shooting up a prayer first for guidance, I was given these words, "I love to encourage people to find a God who knows and loves each one of them by name."

The words tumbled out in front of everyone.

When this happened I was made instantaneously aware that around this table was support, like a family.

People were cheering me on.

I felt it.

They could sense what was happening.

Jeff continued to talk to me, listen, and cook and serve all of us.

Then I asked him, "How long have you lived in Memphis?"

With that question came much disclosure.

"I have only been here a few months. Moved here from New Orleans where my mother lives." He hesitated for a moment and then very succinctly said, "I believed in God once long ago when I was a small boy."

I knew now why I was in that restaurant.

I began to pray for God's words.

"Do you mean there was a time that you believed in Jesus?"

"Yes, he replied, continuing to cook and serve the main course to everyone at the table.

"Why do you not believe now?"

"I don't know but I do know this. I received a head injury while living in New Orleans during a fight. It was so severe that I was not supposed to live but as you can see I did."

At this point I remarked, "So you are telling me that you are a miracle and I am telling you that God has a plan for your life. You matter to Him. He knows about you."

He shrugged his shoulders at my statement.

People were praying at that table for me.

I felt their prayers.

By now he had to take the dishes away for the dinner was coming to a close.

As he walked toward the kitchen, my mother said, "Billie go get your book and give it to him."

I knew I was to do just that.

As I left to go to the car, the mother in the family to my right said, "We were praying for you every moment as you shared your faith with him."

The lady on the left told my mother almost the same thing as I was coming back into the restaurant to pay the bill.

I looked at this college-age young man and said to him, "Jeff, I want to give you my book. It's about opening a window of assurance each day and finding God waiting for you. You need to come back to your faith, feed it by studying God's word, get involved in a church and began to seek out the plan He has for your life."

He thanked me and asked me if I would be having any book signings in Memphis in the near future. I told him that I would have one in three weeks at Barnes and Noble. I gave him the date, thinking to myself, he won't show up. But he did on that day, with his book in hand.

I had some time to share with him my journey of faith.

He received.

Friends came in.

Books got sold that day.

I received.

I gave his name to a man in our Bible class at church and he was invited to a Bible study.

Every day we can choose to see God or get lost in our own disappointments.

We will have them.

"When we fail to choose, we choose to fail...." God designed us to move through time with intentionality" (Note 2)

Hope was watered.

For Jeff and for me.

God knows what He is doing with us.

"Now what I am commanding you today is not too difficult for you or beyond your reach. It is not up in heaven, so that you have to ask 'who will ascend into heaven to get it and proclaim it to us so we may obey it?' Nor is it beyond the sea, so that you have to ask, 'Who will cross the sea to get it and proclaim it to us so we may obey it?' **No, the word is very near you; it is in your mouth and in your heart so you may obey it."** (Note 3)

"Give ear to my prayer, O God...." (Note 4)

He did.

He waters our gardens because He cares for us.

He is preparing us for some divine moment.

Every time we seize it, Hope is watered.

He promises to give us hope.

A divine moment is the next one.

God is in it.

PONDER POINT:

- Why do we fail to experience hope?
- Can God take discouragement and turn it into encouragement with obedience?
- Have you missed a divine moment because you were not available?

PRAYER POINT:

Gracious Father,

We fail because we become inward. We forget that YOU are there watching and caring. The enemy of our souls wants us to withdraw when discouragement knocks, but You, Lord, are training us to be quickened, to respond—to see YOUR Hand when opportunity presents itself.

Your Presence always turns things around.

Grow us into seekers.

Water our hope every day as we journey toward You.

Prepare encounters for us, which will reveal your love.

Water the seed of purpose.

Shower it with possibility.

Save us from ourselves.

Our dreams are too small.

Enlarge our heart.

Our Hope is in YOU.

5
Discovering Faith

Faith is found.

It was a typically gray overcast Norfolk day on the Norfolk Naval Base.

A chill was in the air.

The smell of rain was pungent as gusts of wind whipped up against the ships docked alongside the pier.

Anyone standing there knew squalling weather was coming.

I was one of them.

I had come to say goodbye to my husband, Captain Roy Cash, the Commanding Officer of the USS El Paso, an amphibious cargo assault ship leaving for a Navy deployment.

Deployments involve weeks stretching into months in which the serviceman is at sea and his family is left behind.

They represent the sacrifices required of military families.

Roy had asked me to be there, to watch the ship leave.

In various other commands I would say goodbye at the base or at the pier, driving away before he actually left.

It seemed easier to bear.

This time was different.

He wanted me there.

As I stood on the dock my heart was filled with a knowing grief.

I knew what it would feel like.

I had done this so many times and every time it was consuming.

Questions floated around in my head.

When would I see him again?

What were his challenges?

How would I get through the long months ahead?

How would we change?

It was September, the beginning of fall.

A new school year was about to begin.

Carey, our son, was 15 years old.

Always, I felt an overwhelming loss when Roy would leave to go to sea.

Responsibility and raw regret would crouch behind the door of my mind.

Could I have done anything to make his life better, created a sweeter memory?

The days before he left were filled with trying to crowd too much into too few hours and there was never enough time to say all that I wanted to say.

Today, it was as if a dam broke inside me.

Rushing waters overtaking me.

Every time.

Would I ever get used to this?

Today, I tried to look brave.

As the ship began to pull away from the pier, I glanced up at my precious husband, standing tall and exuding authority on the bridge.

He began to wave and blow me a kiss.

I waved back.

Façade of duty,

Feet of clay,

Fearful.

That was me.

Suddenly one of those blowy gusts nearly knocked me off my feet and I was made aware that there was no one else on the pier with me.

I was alone.

Everyone else had said their goodbyes and was gone.

I felt alone.

Within seconds after the cold wind of isolation hit me I saw out of the corner of my peripheral vision a youthful looking wife with two small children running frantically toward the pier as if to capture in her mind's eye the last picture of her husband's home away from home.

She stood there with tears streaming down her face and I joined her.

The wind was brutal and rain was coming down now.

I noticed that the children had only summer flip flops on their feet and neither she nor either of them had jackets.

It was getting cold.

I asked her if she would like to come and get in my car, so we could escape the howling wind.

She accepted.

We watched the ship as it sailed out of sight, slipping over the horizon.

The heater in the automobile made the unbearable bearable.

There was an unspoken bond and a silence that was deafening for us both even with the noise of children's chatter.

We did not know one another,

And yet we did.

Our emotional pain, common ground and hurt united us.

We were sisters.

I asked her to allow me to pray with her.

She said, "Yes."

And then it happened.

I discovered faith.

It had been planted as a seed long ago in my heart's garden.

Whatever you plant comes up when you need it.

As I finished praying, we said goodbye and then the autumn rain came in strong sweeping waves that washed over me, blinding me.

I strained to see out of my car windows as I started the engine.

The windshield wipers worked hard to clear my view of the road home.

God was teaching me to lean into His showers.

My faith would grow.

I was not alone.

> "Give me, O Lord, a fear of which I may not be afraid."
> **—John Donne**

In his book, *Devotions*, John Donne, the nineteenth century poet, wrote about his fears. He describes his life as being nailed to a bed. Through a potentially life-threatening illness, his confusion begins a search for faith, a "Why me?" questioning.

His writing reveals a dialogue with God about his circumstance.

How familiar.

"Obsessed, he reviews every biblical occurrence of the word *fear*. As he does so, it dawns on him that life will always include circumstances, which incite fear: if not illness, financial hardship, if not poverty, rejection, if not loneliness, failure. In such a world, Donne has a choice: to fear God or to fear everything else." (Note 1)

Feeling alone does not make us alone.

Calamity in life does not separate us from God.

Fear must be faced.

Praying is a way of acknowledging fear and discovering faith.

"Who can separate us from the love of God. Shall trouble or hardship or persecution or famine or nakedness or danger or sword?" (Note 2)

In crisis, the investment of our life comes forth.

God wants our faith in Him to grow.

He wants us to discover more of Him.

He does so out of love.

"Love is doing what is best for someone. But making self the object of our affections is not best for us. It is, in fact a lethal distraction. We were made to see and savor God." (Note 3)

The advantage of looking inward is to discover what is there.

God was birthing a dependency upon Him that would train me to love Him more.

I needed purpose.

Surely He was arranging my way.

I needed to find my faith,

Our entire life experience is an equipping for something He has in mind.

There would be years ahead for me, of separations to endure, children to raise and motivate, people to encourage and faith to grow.

There would be more cold and rainy days, ballgames, missed birthdays and holidays.

But my God never missed a one.

There were times I wished I could run away.

Overwhelmed.

But I didn't.

I began to seek after Him.

In David Baldacci's book, *The Christmas Train,* a writer named Tom was running away from a relationship that he now knew years later was love.

Her name was Eleanor.

He had decided to write a piece about life on a train and the holidays were the right time to pull out the past and take a look.

Why?

Because it gave him uninterrupted thinking to ponder and sort out the mystery of all the "Whys?"

Why did Eleanor leave?

Why didn't he go after her?

Where is she now?

We all have "Whys" in our lives.

Tom was a student of Mark Twain who loved trains and he knew the pull of creativity and the space for introspection would be a worthy combination for a writer.

It was.

Unbeknownst to him, Eleanor was on that train.

He explained the adventure this way:

"It's not getting from A to B. It's not the beginning or the destination that counts. It's the ride in between. That's the whole show." (Note 4)

That's where we differ.

Learning how to live *on the ride* between is the direct result of the beginning with the view of the end in sight.

Faith must have a beginning.

Fears are dealt with *on the ride* in between by a God who is the Conductor.

He drives the train and He has a destination in mind.

The trip is not the whole show.

It is where we are and it is where there are faith discoveries every day.

Tom and Eleanor found love again and the fear that had kept them

apart was dissolved.

Ships, planes and trains return.

And so did The USS El Paso.

Fear returns, but when faith has been planted, it cannot dominate.

Faith supplants it.

"...for everyone born of God overcomes the world." (Note 5)

We are not alone.

God is growing us.

"Let us draw near with confidence to the throne of grace, that we may receive mercy and find help in time of need." (Note 6)

From *Echoes of Eternity, Volume II*, Hal Helms speaks.

"My dear son, you are troubled about many things—and about one thing: your fear of what lies ahead for you and your ability to cope with it. You do not have to cope alone...let the promises work for you. Do not negate them by refusing to believe." (Note 7)

Live in the present.

God is always present.

Are we present to Him?

"The eyes of the Lord your God are continuously on you from the beginning of the year to the end...." Deuteronomy 11: 12

Another discovery of faith.

You are not alone.

Your God cares.

Believe, and faith will flower.

PONDER POINT:

- Have you had a discovery of faith lately?
- Why do you fear embracing the present?
- Can you trust His plans when they don't make sense?

PRAYER POINT:

Almighty God,
I submit my way to you.
You are always waiting for me.
Is it possible to live with such faith?
I think it is if I will get out of the way.
Fear sideswipes me.
Circumstance suffocates me.

It is true that nothing can separate me from your love.
Praying these words builds my confidence.
I want to run toward YOU every day.
Forgive me for my failure to trust.
Order my steps Lord,
Grow my faith.
I want to depend on YOU.
I AM NOT ALONE.

Deny

Oh, how powerful is the pure love of Jesus, which is mixed with no self-interest, nor self-love.

Thomas áKempis

6
Strengthening the Root

Nurture is necessary.

Roots need feeding.
So does faith's flower.

Every time I feed my garden plants, watering them immediately, I do so hoping that the food will make its way downward quickly.

Sometimes a storm blows in unexpectedly and then a deeper feeding happens.

The nutrients find their way to the root.

The root, being the foundation, must always be continually nurtured.

God knows the condition of our root of faith.

In August of 1998, we moved in to a new home in Cordova, a suburban area of Memphis.

The stifling summer heat of a Memphis summer did not deter us.

There is always much to do in moving but this time there were renovations to complete.

Every room would have to be repainted.

This is no small task.

Bookcases were going to replace an existing wet bar in the living room.

This alteration would also give us an extra two feet in the laundry room, which was behind the wet bar.

A patio needed to be turned into a sunroom.

Furniture for the sunroom began to arrive within a couple of weeks and now occupied the living room along with the living room furniture.

We had stuff on top of stuff to do, to think, to organize and accomplish.

A great excuse for dust and a definite housecleaning break.

We know how to move.

Thirty-two moves in Navy life have made us pretty adept.

In about ten days, our homes always looked like we had lived there a long time.

While renovations were going on, the pace slowed and our focus had to be more deliberate each day.

It's fascinating how much we think we control.

A telephone call from my doctor telling me that I need to make an appointment for a breast biopsy proved how much control I had.

None.

Apparently the comparison of last year's mammogram slides with this year's had revealed a disparity.

A small mass showed up that was not there last year.

It might be calcification

Or something more serious.

I was immediately disquieted.

My compulsive decorator's instinct ceased.

It had been a month since the mammogram so I assumed all was well.

All was not.

Moments in life sabotage and force us to search for the root of faith.

Where is it?

Is it intact?

Does it need strengthening?

Will we believe He is in it?

And God watches to see how we respond.

I was scheduled to go into the hospital in about ten days for a needle biopsy to be performed under anesthesia.

My obsession for order stopped.

My need to be affirmed began.

My faith had to find its way to the root.

Crisis always reveals where we are in the faith journey.

For the next several days I asked God to prepare me for the unknown.

I read scripture, internalizing its truth.

I worshipped with inspiring music, singing my assurance in Him to Him.

I prayed, "Lord, should I tell some special friends to pray about this or should I just keep it to myself?"

My impression was, "Yes, ask others to pray."

My brain began to dialogue with my soul.

I am not the first one this has happened to—or the last.

David spoke to his soul, *"Why are you downcast, oh my soul? Why so disturbed within? Put your hope in God."* (Note 1)

My questioning mind continued the debate.

Go it alone or call in the army?

I called in the army, the praying friends I love.

As long as I was actively pursuing my God moment to moment, I had peace.

When I was doing other things, fear crouched in the corners of my mind.

I pondered the change that would come if the results were bad news.

I bargained with God.

He listened.

To obey God is to keep believing, a choice to believe, a conscious choice.

When we impart faith, fear is reduced.

Fatigue had accumulated from the days of readying my home, and I knew I must be rested for the procedure.

I had told Roy my concern.

I felt if I did not get enough rest, I might go in, take the medication, go to sleep and wake up in heaven.

It really would have been all right.

Exhaustion does a mind game on us.

I was tired.

There's a dangerous kind of tired where you don't care.

I was perilously close.

I prayed the night before surgery for God to seal my subconscious mind by His Spirit and to protect it from evil.

Roy stayed awake most of the night praying for me to sleep.

When one wakes from sleep to reality, the mind responds.

The first words that formed were these: "Curse God."

I sensed storm clouds gathering.

Immediately I shouted, "I know these words are not from God. I will never curse my God. He is Jehovah Jireh, Nissi, Elohim, and Rapha. He is my God, my Lord and Savior. The names of a God I know. He loves me!"

And instantly my root was strengthened.

Oh, those names which encompass life, creative force, provider, healer, the list is omni- endless!

All the way to the hospital, I continued to proclaim to God my love and trust.

At 7:00 AM we checked in and a delightful African-American nurse was at the front desk talking about her son Jeremiah with another nurse.

Upon hearing his name, I asked her if she was a Christian and she said, "Yes ma'am, I am."

Behind her desk were these words in a frame:

"Trust in the Lord with all your heart. Lean not unto your own understanding. In all ways acknowledge him and he will direct your paths." (Note 2)

"Thank you, Lord. You are here." I prayed.

God was directing my day.

To obey is to walk where he leads us.

The next thing that happened was the introduction to a pleasant older nurse whose job was to put me in a wheelchair and deliver me from Methodist Hospital to UT Bowld, where a doctor would insert a needle to pinpoint the area in question. We would then return to Methodist for the biopsy. This dear nurse wheeled me across a walkway, connecting the two hospitals, configured like a bridge over Union Avenue.

As she walked and wheeled me, we talked.

Cars were whizzing by in the early morning traffic beneath us. Her first words to me as we began were, "Mrs. Cash, God is so good."

I almost jumped out of my skin at the affirmation.

I was strengthened again as we discussed a faith rooted in a loving God.

We arrived at the office in UT Bowld and I met the first doctor.

He began to tell me about the risks.

I began to tell him about the army of prayer warriors. He gave me a smile said, "Mrs. Cash, I too, am a Christian."

With that, in went the needle, finding its mark with only a slight pressure of discomfort.

Oh, the Grace of God!

Taken back to Methodist, anesthesia was administered and shortly I was brought into the operating room.

My surgeon was having difficulty finding a vein.

She knew I was praying.

After three attempts, she said, "Mrs. Cash, we need a vein."

I remember praying out loud, "Lord she needs a vein. We overcome by the Blood of the Lamb and the Word of testimony."

I heard her say, "I've got it. "

That was the last thing I recall.

It was almost a week before I got the report.

The area was benign, but my faith was positive.

My root was in place.

In fact, it found a deeper level, fed by belief, forced by circumstance to go to the root.

Paul prayed for the Christians at Ephesus that they would be *"filled with the fullness of God"* (Note 3) and that God would bless and strengthen them *"with might through the Holy Spirit."* (Note 4)

Every time we obey God, we become stronger.

Every time we ask for help, He gives it.

Every time we overcome, the world watches and is encouraged.

Along our journey if our eyes are opened, we will see the love of Jesus in all that surrounds us.

He speaks peace to our soul.

"If you faithfully obey the commands I am giving you today...I will send rain on your land, both autumn and spring rains...." Deuteronomy 11: 14a

Storms bring absorbing rain.

Autumn rain is needed.

It is the rain of abundance born of a heart seeking God.

"For the eyes of the Lord range throughout the earth to strengthen those whose hearts are fully committed to him." (Note 5)

Responsible faith has purpose.

It is committed.

We see it in the lives of obedient servants who have learned to trust.

We must become responsible in our faith.

A few years ago I attended a gathering in Nashville, Tennessee with a large group of concerned citizens who had come to our state Capitol to pray for our nation.

We had met legislators and walked the halls learning about our elected representatives and their challenges.

Visiting the rooms where our state laws are made, we prayed for these who were in authority.

After lunch we were looking over the program for the afternoon and wondering how long it might be.

Thinking about the drive home and starting to decide when we should leave, a restlessness developed.

Some were going to leave earlier than others.

As we looked up from our conversation, we saw a very distinguished gentleman approaching the stage.

Dr. Reed, President of Trevecca College in Nashville, was introduced as our next speaker.

When he came to the microphone he spoke these words:

"I thought we might sing a bit to refresh us. One year ago today, I was in a hospital bed with a serious liver condition.

In fact, I was in a coma. Word went out over our campus that I needed prayer for a miracle. I was told that students began to drop to their knees where they were and call out to God for me.

It was so humbling.

In the minutes that followed the call to prayer, out of the coma, I began to sing, *Tis So Sweet To Trust In Jesus.*

At the time of their praying and my singing, my liver began to reverse itself.

I am here today to acknowledge this Mighty God who hears our prayers and delivers.

I stand before you to sing His praise."

Then in a rich baritone voice, *Tis So Sweet To Trust In Jesus* rolled out of his mouth and we breathed in faith, joining him.

In seconds, we were standing, applauding, weeping, rejoicing and then we were singing his song again as one voice unto One God.

I will never sing that song without recalling what God did in this man's life through praying people and a rooted faith.

Buoyed, strengthened, made ready.

We had witnessed a life so filled with purpose that, fresh out of a coma, he could sing about what his life's investment had been: trusting Jesus.

That's a rooted faith.

"The texture of this dimension of faith has everything to do with character. It's about trusting God's character and God testing your character. That's why you cannot speak about faith without talking about obedience." (Note 6)

Visible flowering faith fed by the hand of God was evidenced.

"Certainly not every divine moment is filled with a spine-tingling miracle within in it, but every moment is filled with divine purpose" (Note 7)

And once more the root of ours was strengthened.

A responsible faith takes up its cross and trusts...period.

When a life in Him is so revealed to us, our desire to be responsible grows and we are strengthened.

I wonder, could He use you and me?

PONDER POINT:

- Was there an experience in your life of such anxiety that you wondered if God was there?
- Did you discover the root of your life?
- How does someone else's story strengthen your faith?

PRAYER POINT:

Precious Father,

You were there beside us; We forgot.

We looked at circumstance and tried to figure it out.

We could not.

You looked at our character and saw spiritual neglect.

Darkness fell.

There was no feeling to hold on to,

Only YOU.

Calling us to walk in faith and to obey,

You were there to hold on to.

We discovered YOU again in a fresh way and our faith was strengthened.

We are fickle, pretentious, controlling, trying to orchestrate our own answers.

We cannot breathe life into the root. But You can.

It is in YOU.

When we do let go, YOU come.

YOU, oh Lord, are established forever.

Remind us to find our focus each day.

Feed the root of faith and we will grow.

We want a responsible faith. You are enough.

Pruning the Vision

Discipline grows faith.

Our quarters on the Norfolk Naval Base were small but endearing.

We moved there when Carey went off to college at The Citadel.

It was the home God prepared for us when downsizing became necessary.

We were empty nesters now.

An enclosed front porch wrapped around this quaint but roomy two-bedroom cottage with rose bushes, which swept across the front.

Hardwood floors and a spacious living room made it an inviting place to live.

There was an old-fashioned charm.

You sensed it the moment you stepped inside.

But the rose bushes needed help.

They were six feet tall from gross negligence,

Sprawling, tired, drooping over as if they had finally given up,

Past occupants had given no tender loving care.

The roses were spent.

I wondered what I could do to revive them.

A gardening friend came over and told me to cut them back to about 18 inches from the ground.

"Isn't that too drastic?" I asked. "Can they survive such a severe pruning?"

She laughed and said, "You won't believe them in the spring. Just do it."

In their present state they were alive but not producing much except for tiny fragile flowers intermittently dispersed on every other tangled branch, struggling to bloom.

It was as if the very presence of these sparse pitiful blossoms were trying to acknowledge, "Yes, in spite of my condition, I am still a rose."

Obviously a dramatic measure was called for.

They had never been pruned.

The day we cut them down, it was quite a mess.

No small task.

There were eight of these bushes.

Pruning roses is crucial to growth, quality and beauty.

Flowering plants must be revived periodically.

And so must we.

Our spiritual lives must be emptied regularly of self-interest if we are to develop God consciousness.

Sometimes great pruning must occur.

We cannot stand still.

We cannot remain neutral.

And our Creator knows this.

When greatly pruned, the things we love are exposed.

He unearths our true desires.

To grow spiritually, we must know what we love.

In February, 2003, our son, Lieutenant Carey Cash, a US Navy Chaplain attached to the First Marine Division, Fifth Regiment at Camp Pendleton, California, left for Kuwait and eventually Iraq.

Our daughter-in-law, Charity, was left behind with five children: Caleb, Justice, Phoebe, Nathanael and Ella Joy, ranging in age from eight to two years old.

Raising a family is a tremendous undertaking.

I was able to be in California for about ten days during that month so it was a gift to me to be with her and the children.

The telephone would ring constantly and wives would share helps of all kinds, fears, recipes and friendship.

They encouraged one another and made themselves available to each other.

It steeled them for the moments of bad news ahead of them.

That's what military wives do.

They become family.

I understood that role because it had been mine.

It was incredible to hear Charity voice hope and be a "mother" to others.

She was a cheerleader.

Five little ones of her own to mother at home is a big enough job in itself.

God was teaching dependency to all of us—again.

We needed pruning.

My grandchildren call me Honey, so Honey gathered her grandchildren together one morning around the breakfast nook in the kitchen.

Mom cooked eggs and bacon, Honey cooked up a batch of hope, understanding and love—God's Love.

We talked about the sacrifices that Dad and other fathers were making and how we could help.

They shared their child-like fears and longing for Dad.

Caleb with his intense searching look said, "I really miss him."

Justice squirmed in his chair and said, "I do too."

Nathanael, who was three years old, smiled a big contagious smile and said, "…Miss Daddy."

Phoebe surveyed the group and in her careful but observing way said, "we all miss Daddy."

Ella looked around and smiled at me with her deep dimples showing and said, "Me, too."

I talked to them about what it was like in the Viet Nam years when Poppy, their grandfather, went to war, left Aunt Kellye and their dad behind with me.

Indeed we had experienced separation many times as a Navy family.

They listened and understood a great deal.

I told them that letters would eventually come in the mail.

I suggested they could have a box, keep the notes, taking them out and re-reading them whenever they felt lonely.

I asked them to try and be patient because Dad was far away.

The mail would be slow in coming but it would come.

In turn, they could draw pictures and send them to daddy when Mom sent packages.

Then I said to these precious faces that were in earnest conversation, "We can all pray for him. That will be the greatest gift because Daddy is going to be sharing with the soldiers how much God loves them. He will talk to them about Jesus' love."

When I said the name, Jesus, a knowing look spread across their faces because Daddy had shared about Jesus' love many times with them.

We then prayed for Daddy together.

His children knew how to pray.

It was a good breakfast and afterwards, Phoebe and Ella got up and danced to one of the tapes of Carey singing to them.

He had recorded all kinds of tapes.

There were Bible stories as well and lots of personalized messages of love that he purposed to leave them.

After the children scattered, some outside, some to their rooms, Charity and I hugged and wept together.

God is in every circumstance of our lives.

There is a cost involved in living for Jesus.
Love costs.

The Cross of Jesus represents His cost for us, the shedding of his blood as a sacrifice for our sin.
Perfect sacrifice, once and for all.
Why?
Because of Love.

His is the only love that endures.

"He is good. His loves endures forever." (Note 1)

Sacrifice is required when liberty is denied.
Our military goes to war when freedom is threatened.
They are willing to be the sacrifice.

I saw the impact of this principle in the faces of my grandchildren and it was evident wherever I went on that base.
Families pulling together,
Young men training to go.

God was watching with eyes of love.
There is purpose in everything God allows.

> "There is nothing, no circumstance, no trouble, no testing that can ever touch me until, first of all, it has come past God and past Christ right through to me. If it has come that far, it has come with a great purpose." **—Alan Redpath**

Dependence upon God.

We must learn it over and over again.

Storms are always gathering momentum on someone's horizon.

They do a work in our lives.

"You must learn to live with the insecurities and then ambiguities of life. But know this: I am secure. I am certain. I am not ambiguous. In the storm, I am your Rock that cannot be moved. I am your God." (Note 2)

"Oh Lord, I pray Thee, open his eyes that he may see." (Note 3)

We must find a way to see God in the storm.

That's vision and God is always moving us toward sight.

To see Him I must love Him.

There would be days of anguish ahead for us all.

Months earlier my husband, Roy, and I had planned to go on a cruise to celebrate our fortieth wedding anniversary, not realizing that our son would be headed into a war while we were headed out to sea on a celebration voyage.

We were going away to remember what God had done for us through the years.

Our son was going away to reveal God's love to our soldiers.

We both needed vision.

The ocean opened up our senses, drawing us to the Creator's Heart.

The constant movement of the water reminded us of the movement of His love calling out. An ever-present love.

The sounds of waves lapping against the sides of the great ship cushioning the night held us and awakened the day with promise.

But our souls were being tendered for a new place not found on our itinerary.

These few days were a backdrop, a respite given to us for the stormy days ahead.

We drank in the sunshine and reflected, enjoying what God had provided.

In our hearts great clouds of anxiety were beginning to gather.

A storm was coming.

One morning after a time of quiet meditation and a leisurely walk around one of the decks, I stumbled upon the preparations for an art auction.

There were magnificent pieces by Salvador Dali and Peter Max, a wonderful variety of interesting works by Kinkade, Torkay, Le Kinff and others known in the world of art but unknown to me.

Art represents a slice of life, an artist's statement.

Looking around at the tremendous collection, I felt immediately drawn to attend.

Back I walked to the cabin to tell Roy.

We made plans to go.

It would be a pleasant way to spend part of the afternoon.

Indeed it was.

Observing the process of bidding was fascinating; plus we enjoyed the art.

To our surprise we won two pieces.

The expense of the finer pieces was staggering to the imagination but we were elated over our good fortune.

We were supposed to be there.

Then we saw it. A signed piece by Pat McManus grabbed our souls.

It was a portrait of a stalwart eagle with wings fully spread, soaring above the clouds, which had muted shadings of gun-metal gray fading into subtle hues of ocean azure blue, then billowing at last into a variegated earthy green.

The colors flowed together luminously in a pattern of camouflaged stripes like a great flag interrupted by streaks of sunlight constantly breaking through.

A spellbinding artistic rendering of courage.

A weight fell on my chest and tears sprang to my eyes.

Roy and I looked at each other.

We breathlessly waited for the bidding to begin.

No one bid.

Except us.

It was the last piece they had aboard in the collection of this artist's work.

Then we heard the name of the piece.

"Above the Clouds."

We knew it was meant for us.

This powerful image of a soaring eagle was a reminder of the equipping of God Almighty over our son as he was led into harm's way.

Carey would be in the storm but he would also be ABOVE.

God's love would break through and enable him to soar.

Why?

Because he was engaged in the work of God.

"Until you can see the work of God in the worst circumstances you have not yet seen your life from the eyes of God." (Note 4)

We would see the work of God in this dark night of the soul.

For that is precisely where we were headed.

God loves us and if we are His, He expects us to love what He loves.

God loves people, all people.

"Love does not seek its own private, limited joy, but instead seeks its own joy in the good…of others. In this way we begin to love the way God does. He loves because He delights to love." (Note 5)

"I am the Lord, who practice steadfast love, justice and righteousness in the earth; for in these things I delight, says the Lord." (Note 6)

We knew Carey was called to minister.

We knew he would not carry a gun, no weapon except the Word of God.

We knew there would be risks.

The turmoil in Viet Nam had been ours and we remembered the sting.

Never had we sent a son to war.

There were days in which time hung low upon our shoulders like a shroud.

Breathing didn't feel normal.

It seemed suspended sometimes, suffocating, and irregular.

Not solid and autonomous as usual.

A picture of a soldier, a news clip, a flag waving, sounds of war.

There was little communication.

The first time we heard his voice, it was from a phone call.

He left a taped message because we were not at home.

Oh, how our hearts broke.

Torment knocked.

He tried to sound positive, upbeat but the noise of communication connections thousands of miles away distorted the sound of his voice.

It was like listening in slow motion, garbled sometimes, indistinguishable.

Unbearable.

A few words could be made out, "Mom and Dad, this is your son. I'm OK." And then suddenly no words and then a few more, "Keep praying." And then he was gone, cut off with no resolution, no ending.

No chance to respond.

No chance to say, "I will, son."

No chance to say, "I love you."

I fell on my face with a sense of heavy hopelessness,

And my soul entered its dark night.

We played that tape over and over again just to hear his voice—if only for seconds—for four months. It possessed a pang that haunted me and ran to the hollow place deep inside that needed to be filled with hope.

I found hope on my knees every morning as I cried out to God for this son's life but also for all of our soldiers, and God's vision began to lift the veiled fear slowly.

I discovered when I tried to go through an ordinary day, doing household chores like laundry, an unsuspecting heaviness would settle down upon me, weighting my soul.

I could feel all right in one room and then walking into the next, would be sandbagged, sinking again from a pressure...grief.

Grief for Carey, grief for this ordeal, grief for our family's pain, grief for our soldiers and their families, grief for this far away land that was so oppressed.

Grief is loss and it stalked me.

What was this?

Was it a preparation for my own personal horror, a sensitizing in compassion for others or was it just a part of my own dark night?

When I would hear reports of the wounded and the sacrifices of those who lost their lives,

Despair joined grief.

Imagining the mothers and fathers waiting for phone calls.

Having to watch television in order to know where his unit was.

Two letters in a four-month period

Time, cumbrous like a millstone, slowed the cadence of our lives.

Carey sent a request to us for mail to be written to men who had received none.

Names sent on scrap paper of about thirty-five men between the ages of 18-21, young men who were willing to go, defend and die if necessary.

This letter project was complete priority to Carey as their chaplain.

It was a mission.

He asked me to organize people to write.

I did so on the Internet and in churches, schools and civic groups.

Everywhere I went I asked people to write and e-mail names to their friends.

This was now a part of my mission.

God calls us.

We each have a mission.

My heart began to breathe purpose for God's consuming, demanding love was storming the self, the me, the mine.

His pursuing, terrible flame burning away my world of safety, cutting away anything that could not produce His vision.

I would call Charity when an ominous cloud of paralyzing doubt, uncertainty or terror would sweep over me and we would pray, weep and choose to believe God was with us even though we could not always sense His Presence.

Then we would say goodbye and go do the work.

The waves of darkness continued.

"Oh, spiritual soul! When you see that your desires are darkened, your inclinations dried up, and your faculties incapacitated, do not be disturbed. Consider it grace. God is freeing you from yourself. He is taking the matter from your hand. No matter how well these hands may have served you, they are still clumsy and unclean. Never before could you labor as effectively as you can now when you put down your burden and let God take your hand and guide you through the darkness as though you were blind, leading you to a place you do not know." (Note 7)

God was in our darkness.

One day Roy came home from work and told me that he had seen a Marine convoy crossing the desert in Iraq on his computer screen and at that instant, he had to close his office door and weep, so great was the weight of helplessness.

Darkness does descend.

But so does God.

We functioned daily, plodding through as one who refuses to quit, but has all feeling compartmentalized.

Conscious moments in the daytime and through the night whenever I was awakened, I prayed for Carey.

He was never far from me.

And God is never far from us.

How do we know that?

His Word tells us,

"...He is not far from each one of us." (Note 8)

God was watching to see how much I loved and what I loved.

Yes, this was a dark night of the soul for Roy and me.

Shadows are only possible because there is light and His Light will break through.

Other voices pressed us, attempting to drown out our faith.

Worship or worry

Believing or leaving

Hope or isolation

Courage or fear

Voices from the darkness must flee when God clears our vision.

And He does if we do not abdicate our position.

I was scheduled to leave in late March for the Dominican Republic on a mission trip. It had been on my calendar for a year.

Could I go?

Would I go?

How could I go?

When I agreed to this trip a year ago, I did not know I would have a son in war.

But God did.

He orchestrates our way.

"...When God calls us to battle, the opposition will always be greater than the strength we have." (Note 9)

After much prayer, and the covering of authority over me from my husband, we were in agreement that I was to go.

I left to share the love of God with the people whom He had prepared to hear the Gospel in that nation.

I had anticipation and a desire to go but a guarded heart for I carried the weight with me.

I was compelled to go but I knew God would show me how to release this weight that threatened to bury me.

Weights do their work.

God was in the weight given.

He had planned to free me through a new surrender.

As I boarded the plane out of Miami, I had a 1943 edition of an Amy Carmichael book, "Gold By Moonlight" that I had picked up in England at a second-hand bookstore the previous year.

On the second page she wrote, "In 1637, out of much trouble of mind, the Scottish minister Rutherford wrote to a friend: *It is possible to gather gold, where it may be had, with moonlight.* This book is written to any who are walking in difficult places and who care to gather that gold." (Note 10)

I sat down on that plane and prayed this prayer.

"Oh God, speak to me and bring me to a fresh surrender in You."

In this dear book filled with beauty and insight, these are the words He chose that cleared the clouds and lifted my weight.

"So often we darken our woods by sadness over one dear to us whom we long to see relieved or released, and all the time the Lord of Light is shining on that heart, and speaking words that will never be forgotten, and which, handed on to others like a lighted torch, will travel, who can tell how far? We must learn to look on and see the far more exceeding and eternal weight of glory that is being prepared for our beloved…. Do the men for whom the winds were contrary wish they had been spared the storm that brought their Lord to them walking on the sea (or desert) and caused Him to speak that immortal *It is I: be not afraid*? Could we wish to skirt a wood where our Master wanted to give us a word to lighten the dark woods of others? No, not even now, while the pressure is upon us, would we choose, if we might, to escape from this…which worketh that which is eternal." (Note 11)

That was the answer.

When I read those words, I gave up my burden and surrendered.

I placed my son on the altar.

His forever.

Streams of everlasting Love and assurance broke through.

God gave me back my liberty in Him.

And the storm left my soul.

There were still many days of danger ahead.

We had vision once again.

Pruning had produced growth, much like my rose bushes did.

I was still a child of God,

But one with new vigor and focus.

The dark night had been good for both of us for we had been "simultaneously annihilated and immeasurably strengthened." (Note 12)

Our faith had survived.

We would trust God.

There will always be storms;

And gold can be gathered in moonlight, in the desert, in the ICU unit, in the prison, in disgrace, in poverty, in loss—IN HIM.

On May 25, 2003, Carey came home with his unit.

The next day was his thirty-third birthday;

How we rejoiced.

The joy of the Lord was his strength,

And ours.

God had proven that we could live "Above the Clouds."

Can you?

PONDER POINT:

- Have you ever experienced a "dark night of the soul?
- Did you run toward God or away from Him?
- What spiritual need was met by God?

PRAYER POINT:

My God,

You know what YOU are doing in our lives and we must trust YOU.

There will be times that we cannot sense YOUR Presence but YOU will be walking in the dark beside us.

We can choose to believe or choose to relinquish our faith.

Faith is holy ground.

Forgive us when we have failed, caved in, buried our expectation.

You are the great I AM and I AM is not I WAS or I WILL BE.

You are very present,

And so should we be.

Thank YOU for growing our faith, for sending the storm.

The rains will wash away our fear and clear the air of a clouded vision.

We are your children and YOU are our Father.

Prepare us for the next storm by allowing us to praise YOU for this one.

Surely praise solidifies our song of deliverance.

We love YOU and desire to learn.

Teach us YOUR ways and give us a teachable heart.

We will take up our Cross and follow You.

YOU will meet us every time.

Blooming to Serve

Serving reveals love.

In some years a plant will not bloom.
A frustrated gardener has lots to learn.

In the beginning we must do what we know to do: observe, water, fertilize, prune, weed, mulch the soil.
Prepare for blooming.
Other factors may surface.
Perhaps it is in the wrong place in the garden.
Sunlight is required for blooming and there is a minimum amount needed.
Our crepe myrtle tree is a good example.
We were advised by a master gardener who surveyed the landscaping to position it in the only area of strong sun in our shade garden.
The tree needed at least five hours of sun a day.
The gardener who planted it took a risk.
It may or it may not blossom
He knew that resplendent white flowers were the desired result.
Close scrutiny revealed that it got *almost* five hours of sun but that was not enough.

What is interesting is this; the top half budded.

The bottom did not.

Luxuriant at the top,

Barren at the bottom.

The flowering never makes it all the way down to the bottom of the tree.

We discovered this after keeping tabs on it for a couple of years.

I suppose we have settled for half-bloomed because it is too much trouble to uproot and start over.

Therein is a picture of the quandary we face spiritually.

We settle for half-bloom or none.

Discovering purpose should compel us to become servants.

But we tend to reason it away.

It's too much trouble…

Send someone else…

I like my comfort...

I can't because…

I am not gifted…

Yes, I want to serve God

BUT….

And God watches to see how much we love.

He tells us what He will do from His Word.

"…If you faithfully OBEY the commands I am giving you today—to LOVE the Lord your God and SERVE him with all of your heart and with all of your soul, then I will send rain on your land, both spring and autumn rain…." Deuteronomy 11:13-14a

Serving grows out of loving and is planted in obedience.

We don't get it.

A half-bloomed tree is not flourishing, has not reached its capacity.
It is diminished in potential.

God's Word says to serve Him with all of our heart and all of our soul
Why?
Because of love.

All is all encompassing.
Is there anything to which we give our all?
God says, "All."
I must have allegiance to give my all.
Do I have allegiance to God?

I was almost thirty years of age before it dawned upon me that I was
to serve.
Why?
I was a taker, not a giver.
I absorbed like a sponge does, consuming the immediate—for me.
Self-absorbed not God-absorbed.

Obey, love, serve, whom?

When I obey God, I choose Him.
When I love, I give because of Him.
When I serve it is the overflow of a grateful heart to Him, a heart that
knows God's love is to be shared.
I know I am to be thankful but I must demonstrate my gratitude more
tangibly.
Why do I thank God?

Because I have been forgiven and so have you.

Too easily we forget thanksgiving, getting lost in circumstance.
Every time we forget, we lose our delight in Him.

"Rejoice in the Lord always…I will say it again: Rejoice! The Lord is near… Do not be anxious about anything, but in everything by prayer and petition, **with thanksgiving,** *present your requests to God, and the peace of God, which transcends all understanding, will guard your hearts and minds in Christ Jesus."* (Note 1)

So gratitude positions me to remember what God has done for me.
It is the will of God.

"…In everything give thanks; for it is the will of God in Christ Jesus for you." (Note 2)

A thankful heart serves.
Action because of gratitude spells service.
Supply to serve comes from Him.
Energy, time, compassion, love;
There are no leaks in His Love.
There will always be enough.

"May the Lord make your love increase and overflow for each other and for everyone else, just as ours does for you." (Note 3)

A heart filled with gratitude is not about me.
It's about God's Love.
The sin debt is canceled.
We give to others because we are loved.
We ought to be the most joyous, deliberate givers there are.

Why do we fail to give?

Why do we run from serving?

Why does God keep pursuing us?

His heart is for people.

Our whole lives have been urging us on to fulfill our purpose which is loving God more than ourselves and serving His purpose, embracing His heart for people.

"For everything, absolutely everything, above and below, visible and invisible...
Everything got started in him and finds purpose in him..." (Note 4)

He knows who we can become.

Paul knew who he was.

*"Paul, a **servant** of Jesus Christ..."* (Note 5)

He was a servant.

*"I am a **debtor** both to the Greeks, and to the Barbarians; both to the wise and the unwise. So much as in me is, I am ready to preach the Gospel to you that are in Rome also."* (Note 6)

Paul's life was brilliant, with credentials of education, social standing and authority.

He was vehement in his purpose;

Launching attacks consistently against believers, participating in their demise, even watching as a bystander the day Stephen was stoned.

God wanted Paul for Himself.

He wants us too.

It was brilliant, flashing light coming from heaven that incapacitated him, forcing him face down upon the ground.

He heard a voice:

"Saul, Saul why do you persecute me?

Who are you Lord? I am Jesus whom you are persecuting. Get up and go into the city, and you will be told what to do." (Note 7)

He obeyed.

He did get up, sightless.

Passionately and sincerely wrong in his cause-oriented life, but God arranged an encounter.

Paul met Jesus.

It took blinding light to unmask a misdirected zeal.

"For three days he was blind and did not eat or drink anything" (Note 8)

God chose a man named Ananias to minister to Paul.

His sight was restored, his mission affirmed.

"...A chosen instrument to carry my name before Gentiles and their kings and before the people of Israel." (Note 9)

His course was changed that day.

Saul of Tarsus, persecutor of believers became Paul, a servant of Jesus Christ.

He met His Purpose.

Servant, debtor to the most High God—not to just his own religious sect but to the world—all people.

Have you discovered how much people shape the way you think?

Indeed they do in one way or another.

Jesus changed this man's direction.

He changes ours.

Paul had found a redesigned fidelity and was given a monopolizing mandate to follow.

Servants follow.

"The spirit of Christianity is sacrificial service. Its heroes are servants, people who use what they have for the common welfare...it is service with a cross that is peculiar to Christianity...service which the individual renders by offering himself." (Note 10)

However, the word sacrifice is too harsh for many of us.

We tend to place Paul in a unique category because of his intellect and the times in which he lived.

Yes, he was shipwrecked, beaten and put into prison and so we rationalize that this was a reality for those who were the forerunners of faith.

He wrote manuscripts, encouraged believers and presented the Gospel anywhere at any cost.

He ran his race with fervor, not fear;

He triumphed in the midst of storms.

We applaud him.

He is not us.

We say to our selves Paul was called to the Special Forces unit but that's not me.

Compartmentalized faith, that's us.

Safe, small, faint-hearted, a fading flower.

Until a storm hits.

We need a frame of reference, a root.

In a hand-wringing desperation we cry to the God we have almost forgotten,

But One who is near.

It's easy to look at academic folks like Paul and know we don't fit that description.

God also calls the common man, the ordinary folk.

The woman at the well was very ordinary, even lowly.

Who was she?

Not much, a Samaritan.

Jesus asked her for a drink of water.

It shocked her.

She knew the rules.

Jews did not associate with Samaritans. (Note 11)

Maybe we wouldn't either.

Jesus gives her a drink of Living water, telling her about her life, which included five husbands and a man at present that was not.

He said to her, "Whoever drinks the water I give him will never thirst. Indeed, the water I give him will become in him a spring of water welling up to eternal life." (Note 12)

She asked Him for this living water and then ran all the way into the town telling everyone what Jesus had done, begging them to come and see this man.

And they came.

"Many of the Samaritans from that town believed in him because of the woman's testimony, 'He told me everything I ever did'...and because of his words many more became believers." (Note 13)

Do you think her life changed?

Was she ever the same?

Did she find her purpose?

Her service to the King of Kings was born that day.

This pathetic woman who had so demoralized her life now ministers to us from the scripture because she is important enough to be in it.

God used her and He used Paul.

Will we allow Him to use us?

In between these two extreme, we find ourselves.

What will we do with this life of faith?

Will we bury it, compartmentalize it, keeping it secret service or will we share it openly with love to others, this profound life in Jesus.

When we say, "Yes," blooming begins.

One day I said, "Yes," and God changed my course.

"Yes, Lord I will serve with all my heart and all my soul."

That is the answer that begins growing a faith that will flower.

The promise of rain upon our land is sure, spring and autumn rain.

We must have the spring rain in order for faith to sprout and we praise God for that rain of beginning but we desperately need the autumn rain to continue, for it is the harvest rain of abundance.

"Land that drinks in the rain often falling on it and produces a crop useful to those for whom it is farmed receives the blessing of God." (Note 14)

This is faith harvest.

A devoted young mother taking care of her children honors God by believing, staying and modeling her trust in Him when money runs out and so does a husband.

Faith blooms.

A teenager whose faith is on the line is ridiculed because he will not join in where a dangerous excitement calls.

Faith blooms.

A father loses a job and starts to lose faith but finds a promise in God's word and hangs on in belief.

Faith blooms.

A widow trusts God to fill her emptiness and He supplies a precious relationship that becomes a husband unto Him.

Faith blooms.

A hardened criminal on death row finds God's love in the last moments.

He blooms in death.

God is present.

He calls us to be his life in this world, to serve with abandon, joy and love.

We must be ready to serve.

It was the fall of 2002, I was returning from a mission trip to England, my ninth.

God had consistently created in my soul a love for this land.

The Gospel had been presented in every place I had spoken.

Some received, some did not.

There were faces of men and women who exhibited the joy of Christ.

There were anxious countenances bearing vacuous lives.

Each time I spoke God gave me more love, more strength, more faith.

I was always amazed when the time came to go home, that I was not completely spent.

I was not.

Overflowing with thanksgiving and the deep awareness of God's provision was the emotion I carried home.

There was always enough.

I love my friends, Pat and David.

They are true servants.

We awakened to a heavy rain the morning I was scheduled to fly home.

No sun, just low hanging clouds.

A bad dream had jolted me from sleep. I heard the splattering sound of the rain against the windowsills and opened my eyes with a sense of foreboding, risk.

I asked the Lord to wake up Peggy and Beth to pray for my trip home.

How wonderful it is to have such a bond with praying friends that God can wake up to pray.

It was going be a long trip: Southampton to Paris, Paris to Atlanta, and Atlanta to Memphis.

All in all about twenty hours, including the layovers in each place.

I knew God would take care of me.

This trip had been covered in prayer by people who know that intercession is needed for those on mission.

Long ago I understood this principle:

Ministry must have a prayer covering if it is to be empowered.

We got to the airport, said our goodbyes and gave our hugs.

I went through security and was seated in the waiting area when I heard that my flight was delayed.

It did not surprise me for I could still see that we were in worsening weather conditions.

Visibility was nil.

Our small aircraft would have to fly at a lower altitude than usual because of the weather and the brief flight time to Paris was less than an hour.

Because of this the weight of the luggage had to be recalibrated.

Seven people were to be removed from this flight with their luggage.

Too much weight.

Of course there would be a process to determine who they would be.

I began to pray.

If I were to be one of them, God would provide for me some way that day.

He took me to England and He would bring me home.

During the delay, I decided to get a cup of coffee.

However, when I approached the coffee bar in the lounge, I discovered that I only had two euros, two dollars and no pounds.

Not enough for coffee.

No money, no coffee.

I sat down with none after being unable to convince the pleasant, dark haired woman behind the counter to take what I had.

It was not acceptable or not enough.

Opening my Bible I began to read and wait out the flight dilemma.

Shortly the woman came over to me and said, "Excuse me. Could I just give you a cup of coffee?"

I smiled and said, "You sure can."

It was then I detected an accent but was not sure where she was from.

Thanking the Lord quietly, I continued to read.

When she brought the coffee to me I thanked her and then she said, "I would like to ask you a question. Somehow I think it will be okay to ask you."

I nodded and said, "Certainly."

In the next minute she said, " Do you believe that Elvis loved Priscilla when he married her?"

Now I was so taken back for a moment I did not know how to respond.

She was completely serious and did not know that I lived in Memphis or that I had a good "Elvis" story, which I could have told her.

This kind lady was intent and sincere.

While I was pondering my answer, she continued to tell me that she had read about six books about Elvis' life, trying to find out the answer to this question.

I needed a response.

After all she had given me a free cup of coffee.

So I said, "Yes, somehow I do believe they loved each other. Priscilla was a young teen living in Germany with her parents when Elvis met her. He convinced them to allow her to come to Memphis where I live. She graduated from a finishing school. They were married at a young age. From what I have read, they seemed to be much in love at that time."

That satisfied her.

She was delighted, thanking me over and over.

It was as if I had opened a door of mystery and suspense that she had knocked at many times.

Almost immediately, I heard over the loud speaker that seven men had been taken off my flight and we would be boarding soon.

Then it happened.

A spiritual discernment came to me.

It was as if scales fell off my eyes.

Any person who would be that consumed with Elvis needs to know about Jesus.

"Lord, show me something to do, to say to this woman."

I realized that I still had one of the booklet tracts in my Bible, which I had taken with me for ministry events, and I pulled it out.

Over to the counter I went and asked her name, giving her my name.

Her name was Isabella.

She was Spanish.

Every word I needed was given to me.

"Isabella, I have a booklet I want to give you. It is filled with stories of people overcoming difficulties after 9/11 in America. The stories will move your heart for they are stories of faith. When you get to the back of the booklet you will discover that God loves you and has a plan for your life and wants you to know Him personally. I know you will be blessed by this booklet."

She took it and clutched it as though she had found the answer for which she had been searching.

In broken English, Isabella said, "Billeee, Billeee, thank you, thank you. My husband, he leave me this week. We marry when we were young like Elvis and Priscilla and I am desperate and I cry out to God, 'God send someone to me to tell me you love me and Billeee, you are the one.'"

I could not speak.

My flight was called again.

Grabbing the hand of Isabella I said, "Yes, Isabella, Jesus knows your name and He loves you. God bless you."

My heart was pounding.

I was praying.

"Lord, You are the author and finisher of our faith.

I know you arranged this.

Open the door of Isabella's heart to You."

Jesus had come by way of Elvis and a cup of free coffee in another country in an airport because of a delayed flight in an autumn rain.

I could have missed an opportunity to serve.

Now Isabella is in my heart forever.

I have prayed many times for her.

As we lined up to run to the plane, an ominous clap of thunder was heard and rain pelted the passengers all the way up the steps into the plane.

I really could not believe we would take off.

Maybe we were going to just sit for a while on the runway as the storm passed.

The rain was not over and neither was the adventure God had prepared for me.

Finding my seat, I looked out the window as I was praying the prayer I pray before boarding any flight anywhere:

"Father, choose my Captain and first officer and let them be in agreement. Send your angels to check all mechanical parts and if any be defective, do not allow this plane to take off. Oh God, do not allow anyone to enter this aircraft who is bent on destruction. My trust is in You alone. As your child I pray in authority in the name of Jesus and under His Blood."

We all pray when we fear,

But praying with knowledge and authority comes from practice.

We needed prayer for this flight.

Weather was a definite factor but I also knew that God hears the prayers of his children, so I qualified.

As I finished breathing this prayer, a disheveled, unkempt, older lady asked me if this might be her seat which was next to mine. I looked at her ticket and told her that it was. Very tentatively, she sat down. Suddenly she blurted out in an English accent, "I have never flown by myself before and I am so worried because of the rain."

She looked older than she probably was.

I felt compassion for her because she was terrified.

I told her how I had prayed.

She looked into my eyes and said, "I'm so glad I'm sitting by you."

Then I began to explain what happens when a plane takes off relating how the ascent could be turbulent because of wind in rainy weather.

I told her that the pilot would continue to climb until he found a more comfortable altitude at which to fly.

Sounded good.

I was also trying to convince myself that this would happen.

Then I explained that the same process would happen when we descended for landing. Roughness going up.

Roughness coming down.

Just as life is.

We would have about thirty minutes in the air above the storm.

Would you believe the ascent was not bumpy after all?

I could not believe how the sunlight streamed through the foggy layer once we were above.

She told me her story.

Her name was Sue.

She and her husband retired in France, living in a village outside of Paris.

She had been to England to see her aged, ailing mother who was in her nineties in the final stages of Alzheimer's. Summoned to her bedside, she was given the prognosis of this probably being the last time she would see her mother's alive.

Her "Mum" had recognized her.

When she told me this, tears began to stream down her face.

"What a gift God gave you, Sue."

She gave me a queried look and said, "Well, I suppose it was."

An attendant brought rolls by and offered them to us.

Sue wondered if she had to pay for them.

She really had never traveled alone.

I told her they were free;

Free rolls, free coffee.

We sipped coffee and God stirred faith into our conversation.

In just a few moments I knew why I was sitting next to her.

She needed the Love of God in her life.

Time was running out; we were starting our descent already.

Once again, no bumps.

I went to pull out my booklet and my boarding passes fell out as well.

Looking over them, I caught my breath as I realized that I had been given a wrong boarding pass. It was for a flight from Paris to Atlanta but for one that had already left. Attached to the back of it was a boarding pass for some poor man who was to go to Milan, Italy and was probably wandering around the airport because he had no boarding pass.

I had it.

How in the world this happened I do not know.

I remember looking at mine and seeing Paris to Atlanta.

I did not look at the time.

When I saw the mistake, I said to Sue. "I will have to have my boarding pass changed because it is incorrect and I also have someone else's by mistake."

She looked wide-eyed and asked, "What will you do?"

I told her that God would take care of it and work it out and then began asking Him to do so inside my head.

Then she said, "Billie, I do not know how I will get across this big airport and find my way to the train station."

Her hands were clutched.

I replied, "If God could seat you next to me, surely He can find someone to direct you across the airport and to the train station. Just ask Him."

With a deep expression of possibility, she said, "I will."

Hurriedly I went through the booklet and reminded her that God knew her by name and that He loved her.

She said, "I believe He does."

We landed with out incident and sunlight was breaking through the greenhouse structure of the Paris airport.

We hugged our goodbye.

Off went the little bag lady but there was a lilt to her step.

I proceeded to get in a line for changes to be made with tickets. It was an international experience in every way.

Different languages were being spoken by the personnel serving at this passengers' service desk.

I prayed feverishly about this glitch as I waited.

God would get me home.

I got in line.

An Italian man was ahead of me.

His harried wife, across the walkway with two adorable, mischievous little girls under four years of age, kept trying to talk to him. She was most impatient.

The girls were laughing and running circles around their mother who was not laughing.

He was called to the counter.

I was next.

Two men rushed abruptly to the head of the line when it became clear that I was next to be served. One in particular slammed his briefcase down upon the counter with force and intimidation.

They then proceeded to get in front of me.

An attendant told him to go to the end of the line but he would not.

They were dressed in brocaded flowing robes wearing headpieces,

which were exotic, elaborate.

I tried to appear calm.

Politely but purposefully I said, "Excuse me sir, I believe I am next."

Instantly one of them railed on me and began to speak in his language and attempted to get me to respond in kind, in anger.

I shuddered in fear.

Trembling and shaken, I uttered a prayer in my heart, "Lord what do I do?"

No audible words but a deep and succinct impression came to my mind as an answer.

Do not look at them in the eye.

Do not try to dialogue with them.

Speak my name.

Wow, I thought.

I decided this was exactly what I should do.

So in the next breath, I said, "Jesus" quietly then I repeated "Jesus" clearly but softly and when I spoke it the third time with assurance, I sensed an invisible protective shield falling around me.

I fell encapsulated, secure.

They heard His Name spoken.

They knew that Name.

His Name has authority.

They both simultaneously pulled back from hovering over me and fell silent.

My name was called.

Relief flooded my soul.

My ticket was made right.

I left when I was scheduled to leave and the flight home was uneventful.

Oh, the power of His Name!

JESUS

I shall never forget that day.

But I still was not home.

Arriving in Atlanta, I went to the ladies room, down to customs and on the baggage claim area.

When I got there I discovered I did not have my boarding pass, it had fallen out in the ladies room.

Again I prayed.

This time it was, "Show me, Lord, what the next step is."

When I told my story to the baggage attendants, they sent someone up to the restroom; no boarding pass was found.

I was not allowed to go back through customs.

I am sure that is where I dropped my boarding pass.

An airline attendant listening to this search saga told me that undoubtedly I was in the computer so they should be able to find a ticket number and issue another boarding pass.

This was the day for boarding passes.

My baggage checks, however, were stapled to the back of the Paris-issued pass and standing at the baggage claim, I discovered I had no luggage that had made it from Paris.

I had no claim ticket to prove I ever had any.

Back to prayer.

I was advised to go upstairs and tell my story to a Delta agent.

I asked God to choose her.

He did.

She was kind, helpful and I prayed as she searched the computer for any baggage numbers with my name attached to them.

Finding them in the computer, she gave them to me.

I thanked God.

Now I had numbers, a boarding pass but no baggage.

Calling Roy, telling him I was safely in Atlanta but my baggage was elsewhere, I prepared to board my last flight.

By now weariness cloaked me and the ride to Memphis seemed more like outer space travel.

Exhaustion and jet lag had begun to claim me.

I dreaded going through this saga again at the Memphis airport.

If one's luggage gets left in this country there is much computerized technology available to locate it. I have never had any thing permanently lost here but baggage left in the Paris airport did not offer comforting odds.

When I disembarked in Memphis I had been up twenty hours.

A Delta agent walked toward me and before I could speak, she said, "Is your name Cash?" "Yes ma'am," I replied.

She related, "We have located your bags.

Your two pieces of luggage left in Paris will arrive tomorrow at 7:00 PM." She gave me the flight number and the tracking information.

Now I still had to go through the next day in faith.

I did and at 9:00 PM, my bags arrived at my door, sent on a plane, taken through customs without me, delivered to my home.

I know my Redeemer lives.

He has called me to serve.

Every time I go in obedience, my faith grows.

As a seasoned traveler, I had never experienced an ordeal like this one.

I am sure it will not be the last traveling tale of turmoil for me.

This I know:

Faith bloomed for Isabella, Sue and me.

Lost tickets, lost bags, lost people.

The Bible says, "The lord will fulfill his purpose for me." (Note 15)

I must go.

No half-bloom for me.

PONDER POINT:

- What is your excuse for not serving with your whole heart?
- Do you want your life to bloom with Faith?
- Does it matter what you do with what you know?

PRAYER POINT:

Almighty God;

How I have run away from serving,

But YOU did not run from me.

How I have neglected this area of my faith journey hoping YOU would not notice,

But YOU did.

Where would I be today without Your Love and Divine intervention?

Lost, with no hope, but lots of baggage.

Deliver me from the suitcase of my expectations.

It's too small a world for the God who formed me.

I need to be challenged to live for YOU.

To be your disciple, I must deny my agenda, take up my cross and follow where YOU decide, serving with my whole heart.

I want a Flourishing Faith.

Take Up

Thou hast proved that purest joy is duty.
H. Coleridge

9

Harvest Beauty

Faith grows beauty.

"Oh beautiful for spacious skies for amber waves of grain…."

We sing about the harvest in *"America the Beautiful"* and when we can see it, there is a sense of fulfillment.

Fields of grain are a work of beauty in harvest.

The autumn rain has done its work.

It is not always so.

The farmer plants his seed, irrigates, fertilizes, watches and waits. Some years the abundance is not present, for calamity has struck in severe drought, torrential rains or disease.

Devastated, yes, but he does not quit.

He begins again.

After all, he is a farmer and perseverance is now a part of his character.

The gardener has a similar experience.

Some years the azaleas blossom with such a profusion of loveliness that one knows all the right conditions have been met.

The autumn rain has done its work.

Delight to the heart of the gardener is to behold flourishing beauty in his garden.

Full, ample, resplendent, more, abundant.

That is what he desires.

When we behold a life of faith that has met the seasons, adjusted and continued, a harvest is inevitable.

The autumn rain has done its work.

There is a faith harvest to the righteous.

They have sown the seed, watched and prayed and loved a God of trust and vigilance.

They have not been exempt from the elements of storms.

They have roots that are deeply established and a lifetime of pruning with a clear resolve to serve at all costs.

When we glimpse such a life, we are summoned to higher ground because Jesus is visible as the source of beauty in their lives.

Her name is Wayve.

Life for Wayve began in Minnesota.

Significant women shaped her life.

An Irish mother named Edna and a Swedish grandmother of Godly influence.

A strong and trustworthy father named LeRoy David Nelson was one of three brothers who married three sisters.

Can you imagine having twenty-four double cousins?

What fun.

They must have had family reunions that were off the charts.

But it was also the time of the Great Depression, a lean and severe economical climate.

A time ripe for God to move hearts—and He did.

The Sawdust Trail of revival meetings in tents drew the jobless and discouraged.

They were everywhere.

Money was gone.

Faith was not.

It was waiting to become integral in Wayve's life.

Timing is important to God.

Church was a viable part of her life and music was a strength.

Unfortunately by the time her husband Warren Berg came into her life, Christianity had become a list of negatives, for the rules seemed to outweigh the benefits. Wayve couldn't figure out why she always wanted to "do the don'ts and don't the dos."

The apostle Paul had the same dilemma and so do we.

"I do not understand what I do. For what I want to do I do not do, but what I hate I do." (Note 1)

She just decided to forget about God.

He did not forget about her.

A promise from His Word,

A search for purpose,

A discovery planned by Him,

Understanding began to take root.

"*...Even when I was too weak to have any faith left, He would remain faithful to me. He would never deny Himself.*" (Note 2)

What would those words signify to Wavye?

God was faithful and He was pursuing her.

Warren Berg had a religious bent and felt his family should have some religion.

Just religion.

Religion grows suspicion not beauty.

One day while driving down a freeway listening to a radio broadcast from the Moody Bible Institute station, the wonder and transforming power of Jesus broke into Warren Berg's heart and he had an encounter with the Living God.

Repentance is the work of showing us our sin and turning us around.

Belief in God brought relationship.

At this time Wayve and Warren had two of their four children and she says, "She had to unlearn a lot." Warren started off his spiritual journey with nothing to unlearn.

The words of her courageous father tell the rest of the story. A phone call came in one day and she was told, "Sis, open up your Bible. We have taught you everything wrong."

A husband exchanges religion for real faith.

A father admits wrong teaching and makes it right.

The reading of one little book changed her course. *"The Saving Life of Christ"* by Ian Thomas brought spiritual revelation. In Chapter Five the story of God speaking to Moses from a burning bush was recounted.

"It was not the bush that was important, it was God in the bush. The Romans 5:10 text told me that *'just as I was reconciled to God by the death of his son, much more I would be saved by His life.'* It is His life in me that is important, not what I can do for Him."

That did it.

"Christ in me, the only hope of glory." (Note 3)

Relationship.

Wayve became a child of God.

We seek after Him, not realizing that He is the Divine initiator.

We come to Him from different backgrounds and times but He is always tracking us.

It happens through many avenues, a book, a verse of scripture, and a song of God's grace.

A word fitly spoken.

He brings purpose to life.

The faith journey has a harvest when, consciously, His Word has been planted and new life has emerged.

Spring rain causes a seedling faith to sprout, to come up.

Weak but growing.

We must have it to begin.

Autumn rain produces a faith harvest from a life that has nurtured the Word of God, loved and served Him with the whole heart.

Even then, He promises more.

"...You may gather in your grain, new wine and oil...." Deuteronomy 11: 14b

In spring rain we are becoming established but in autumn rain we are gathering in the fruit of an established faith.

In Wayve's life, Dr. William Berntsen, President of Northwestern College in Minneapolis, Minnesota was the one God chose to encourage her to sing the Gospel. Once again her father came through with advice that produced spiritual integrity. He said, "Sis, be sure the songs that you sing have reached your own heart first because if they haven't, they will never reach any one else's heart."

God had a work for Wayve to do and He had encouragers along the way.

She began to give what she had and a passion for service was heightened.

Music was the first way she shared the Gospel and it took her around the world to Canada, China, Japan, Korea, Israel, Mexico, Singapore, Russia, India, South Africa and to Central Europe and various island countries.

Every step of obedience opened up the path of opportunity.

Joy blossomed.

God added a speaking ministry to her music because a deep love for the Gospel necessitated knowledge and complete dependency upon God's Word.

Leadership/consultant roles evolved in organizations with Christian

Women's Clubs of America, regional management councils, and a variety of college and university boards outreaching to international students.

A flourishing life is the result of simple faith lived out in small ways.

When I met Wayve in Naples, Florida a few years ago, I saw the obedience that marked her life.

She came to an event where I was to speak to several hundred women.

We had dinner together with the committee the night before to pray and fellowship.

I saw her impact.

An articulate and able Bible teacher in her early eighties by now, she was teaching home and church Bible studies to hordes of women who were flocking to hear what God was saying to them through her.

An octogenarian, she had an enriched life of faith, wisdom and insight, longevity with the Lord.

She made the Bible come alive because she knew who had sustained life for her.

Jesus alone.

Spending six months in Florida and six months in Minnesota each year, one might think she would take a break.

Not so.

I went to Minnesota the next year and there she was wherever I spoke.

Full of life, building friendship with others, growing faith, flourishing.

Widowed but not buried, she has a burning heart for God.

There is an entourage who gladly drive her to and from anywhere she chooses.

Driving "Mz Wayve" is privilege.

I can see why.

Touching people with wit, humor and Godly Truth is a powerful way to stay filled up with joy.

Expectant with an eye toward heaven,

That's Wayve.

Her e-mail has a hot pink background and large letters.

She carries God's presence even on the Internet.

Immediately you know whom it is from and it is always filled with the wonder of God.

Aches and pains get no press but prayer does.

A lively mind always taking in and giving out His Word is always producing a fruitful faith.

Ask Jo Anne who worked for Triple A and came to speak on road rage and left with the peace that passeth understanding.

Jesus became real to her.

Wayve would not let go and now she is in Bible study, sharing her faith.

Potential for God.

That's all of us.

But do we use what we have?

Do we give it away?

Do we retire and let someone else do it?

Last Thanksgiving, our daughter Kellye was appearing in *"Joseph and the Amazing Technicolor Dreamcoat"* at Mansion America in Branson, Missouri. Wayve was going to be there to visit her daughter and son-in-law over the holiday and she came to the performance. Her beloved son Bruce, in his early fifties, had suffered a massive heart attack days before and we were in prayer for his life.

Of course the evening was delightful as we saw and experienced the story of Joseph come to life on the stage with the tremendous imagination of Andrew Lloyd Webber's pen. One could have followed along from God's Word and seen first hand the accuracy of the story.

Having seen it many times, as Kellye's mother, I am always moved to tears in the last scene when Joseph is reunited at last with his father, Jacob.

The story is one that reveals the faithfulness of God.

Enduring the jealousy of his brothers who beat and sold him, Joseph was left to die.

Plans for Joseph were in the making.

His Heavenly Father had given him the ability to interpret dreams.

Cast into prison by an unscrupulous, evil woman, set up to fail, he flourished.

His heart grew in beauty towards God.

Joseph possessed integrity.

His ability discovered, he was uncovered as a leader among men and placed in authority by Pharoah the king.

Famine came.

Plenty was found because of Joseph's storehouses filled with grain.

The deceiving brothers came calling for food.

He recognized them.

He loved them.

He forgave them.

The tragedy of His life trained Him for Godly authority.

"...God was with him and had rescued him from all his troubles. He gave Joseph wisdom and enabled him to gain the goodwill of Pharoah King of Egypt; so he made him ruler over Egypt and his entire palace." (Note 4)

In the scheme he conjured to reveal himself to his brothers, he revealed the true self.

Benevolent, compassionate, reconciling.

A reunion was destined with his beloved father.

In the musical, this moment releases emotion, restores hope and gives a glimpse of heavenly finality, which encapsulates the kingdom of God.

Together forever.

God is always arranging life for His own for He knows what it will take to get us ready for our eternal home.

When the show had ended, I saw Wayve in the lobby.

I asked her how she liked it and she said, "It's hard to speak about what I feel."

I knew that the life of her son Bruce was hanging in the balance on earth, but not in heaven.

We had seen a poignant picture of reunion in the story of Joseph and his earthly father.

It was glorious.

Once again God's Word had pointed the way that was to come.

He had prepared her heart for the reunion of Bruce with his earthly father and he entered those portals of eternity days later on December 3, 2003.

His brother Daniel, known as Dino, eulogized Bruce tenderly at the celebration of his life. The other children, Marilee and David, were also present with their families as well. Altogether nine grandchildren, representing the four siblings, came together for this time of expressing love unto God.

"Bruce had his own way of bestowing masculinity. My Dad went to heaven when I was twenty-three years old and his early departure left a large hole in my world. Although I am not sure he ever knew it or was comfortable with it, the mantle of male leadership in our family passed to my older brother Bruce…from that time forward, time spent with Bruce took on a different dimension…I appreciated every minute spent with him…we played. We did stuff…always a time of action, accompanied by those whopper stories he'd tell…. Today the little boy who stood on that sidewalk long ago stands here again squeezing his father's hand in heaven looking across the great expanse that separates me from my brother. I will miss his playfulness, his little boy's heart, his humor, his constant mischief, his sense of adventure, his gifts of time spent with me…. I have no fear…I know where he has gone and I know he will be there to greet me when I follow him as little brothers do. I trust he will tell my Dad and grandparents that I love and miss them. Until we see each other in Glory, I say goodbye for now…I know he travels safe and secure in the arms of God."

His mother Wavye eloquently shared her thoughts that day and her belief based on the Word of God.

It is captivating in its simplicity.

"The wisest man who ever lived on planet earth, Solomon, left us some words to live by in Ecclesiastes, Chapter Three. *'There is a time to be born, a time to die, a time to laugh and a time to cry.'* Our family has laughed, cried and prayed a lot these past two weeks. We have a Godly heritage. Those who have gone before us have left powerful legacies not because they have been good but because they have believed what God has said about where we came from, who we are and where we are going...our trust is in what our Lord has promised.

The Bible, the written word of God is our authority—PERIOD. In the Old Testament God spoke to Moses at Mount Sinai and reminded him of how He had brought the children of Israel out of Egypt. He said, '*I carried you on eagles' wings and brought you to myself.*' My son Bruce loved to watch the eagle soar.

What does this have to do with us who are not Israelites? The promise to us is found in the New Testament in the book of Galatians where we read, 'If you belong to Christ, then you are Abraham's offspring... inheritors of the promise God gave Abraham.' Bruce believed and confessed Jesus Christ when he was a young boy. My wild and wacky first-born son is with God.

How do I know he is in heaven? I know with positive assurance that my son is with God because Jesus hung on a Roman Cross for the sin of the world and said three words, '*It is finished.*' At that moment salvation's wondrous plan was done! There was nothing we could ever do to add to that, nothing we could do to diminish it in any way... Solomon's words assure me once again '*Whatsoever God does, that will be forever...nothing shall be added to it, nothing shall be taken away*'.

On December 3, 2003, God '*carried him on eagles' wings and brought him to Himself.*'

Because of that assurance, '*We sorrow not as those who have no hope*' but rejoice with the Psalmist in Chapter nine who wrote, '*Oh Lord, I will praise you with all my heart, and I will tell everyone about the marvelous things that you do. I will be glad, yes filled with joy because of you. I will sing Your praise. Oh, Lord above all gods.*'"

What beauty in mourning from sheer faith in the Word of God!

The wave of God's Grace given to a Wayve whose life was Grace.

Flourishing faith modeled in a family, lived out, reproduced.

God watched and on that day Wavye Berg Bradley received a faith harvest.

"The glory of God is a man fully alive." —**St. Iraneus**

In life or death, if we are fully alive in Christ Jesus, God is glorified.

All of life grows our faith.

Books enlarged Wayve's life and now she is in one.

Authors stretched her vision of beauty. There were men like Dr. J. I. Packer, Oswold Chambers, Ian Thomas, Ray Stedman and women like Hannah Whitehall Smith.

People enlarged her horizon of service, as did Mary Clark and Helen Duff Baugh of Stonecroft Ministries.

Experiencing God in unusual ways was a gift of favor to her; singing, *"Amazing Grace"* in the Taj Mahal where no one speaks above a whisper, addressing diplomats in India by sharing her faith story in testimony and song, standing and singing praise to God Almighty in the ruins of Israel, all were a part of God's design for this woman.

She had been promised that she would gather in new grain and indeed she has.

" Jesus said to Peter, *'Do you love me?'* and Peter said. *'Lord, you know I love you'* and then Jesus said, *' Feed my sheep'."* (Note 5)

Wayve Berg is still feeding sheep into the late winter season and they are feasting on the grain of the Word of God.

Long after "Mz Wayve" has bid farewell and entered the city called Glory, those seed grains she has planted will continue grow and harvest faith.

Gleaning Truth makes a garden beautiful.

"Real seeking of God involves searching God's word to learn the things that bring Him joy." (Note 6)

She describes herself in words left behind by her precious friend Helen Duff Baugh, "…a woman simple enough to believe God."

Flourishing faith has a harvest when the Word of God is sown and watered.

The Creator sends the autumn rain.

PONDER POINT:

- Why have I neglected God's Word?
- Have I ignored the potential to serve God?
- What must I do now to establish this habit in my life?

PRAYER POINT:

Holy God,
You were there all the time.
I esteemed You NOT but YOU pursued me.
When I was faithless, YOU were faithful.
Praise YOUR HOLY NAME that YOU would not let go.
I long for a Harvest of faith that is beautiful in YOU.
I have neglected your Word.
Forgive me.
Redeem the time I have left.
Give me joy in serving YOU.
Stay near me all the way to Heaven.
Show me the way.
Make me accountable to someone trustworthy.
Urge me to grow the Love of YOUR WORD in my daily life.
I surrender again.
Harvest my faith, Great and Holy God.

10

Harvest Blessing

Faith brings blessing.

Sometimes a gardener wants a challenge.

For me it was the primrose.

I suppose it harkens back to my love for England for they are everywhere and grow so easily most of the year.

In my research I discovered that they require mild temperatures of 45-55 degrees in winter and temperatures of no higher than 80 in the summer.

Memphis is not in the ideal zone for growing them.

I found one variety that blooms in the fall and winter.

Planted in the late summer, it needs the autumn rain to become established.

I also learned that primroses like facing north and enjoy the shade even though sunlight is necessary for the bloom.

They have numerous medicinal uses as well; a tea for headaches and a fine salve for wounds.

Designed for pleasure but made useful.

If they survive into the third year they can be cut back to one half the size after flowering in the fall and can began to flourish in the garden.

Tender Loving care.

Gardeners know how to give it.

I decided to try the impossible.

Planting my first primrose in a partially sunny bed in my shade garden behind the watchful crepe myrtle tree seemed to be the right spot.

It worked.

One morning very early, with dew still present, I tiptoed outside into the garden and there it was.

The primrose plant bloomed with deep violet star-like flowers with a penetrating yellow eye in the center. Lush, green cabbage leaves hugged the ground.

Pristine, one of a kind.

Against the odds it bloomed.

A blessing to the gardener.

God wants to bless us.

"I will bless them...I will send down showers in season; there will be showers of blessing. The trees of the field will yield their fruit and the ground will yield its crops; the people will be secure in the land." (Note 1)

A young woman attending Nyack College, thirty miles north of New York City, wrote her first Gospel song in 1941.

She was to be a blessing to God.

Her name was Beatrice Bush but her friends called her Bea.

On evening while attending a school missionary meeting, Bea heard a visiting missionary speaker, Mrs. J. Van Hine from Viet Nam, relate an account of a communion service in Hanoi. As the communion elements were being served that evening, a pastor in the meeting posed a question. "Has anyone been omitted in the distribution of the bread?" (Note 2)

Deeply moved, Bea wondered how many had been omitted from the distribution of the Bread of Life and off she went to her room composing *"The Breaking of the Bread."*

A call was beginning on her life.

William Bush, her father, was a railroad man with the Lehigh Valley railroad in Waverly, New York but it was music that really had his heart. "My dad could pick up any instrument and play it…. He loved music dearly…I guess he was the one that gave me the push…." (Note 3)

Her mother, Emma Hakes, could play by ear so music was a root in her life.

She thought teaching public school music would be her direction.

God called her to follow Him in ministry.

Bea was to be His blessing.

"For God planted them like strong and graceful oaks for his own glory." (Note 4)

He had planted her faith.

At the age of seven, in a tent meeting, Bea heard about the love of Jesus and opened her heart to Him.

Tent meetings drew the restless and wandering for the great Depression was about to descend. Piano lessons began shortly thereafter, continuing for about five years.

When the Depression finally hit, money ran out.

Hard times grow a hardy people.

Her piano teacher, Mrs. Avis Abell, paid a visit to her parents and told them piano lessons would continue without any thought of payment.

God intervenes when faith is rooted.

He took pleasure in the promise of Bea's life.

His music was to be hers.

What brings Him pleasure?

"Bringing pleasure to God is called worship." (Note 5)

Bea had a hunger for worship.

God had training waiting for Bea.

Attending Houghton, a small Christian college, studying voice and piano until her sophomore year, money once again evaporated.

God did not.

A husband and wife team in a traveling evangelistic ministry, Reverend and Mrs. B. B. Bosworth, needed a pianist/soloist and Bea was the answer.

At this point her ministry in piano and voice was launched.

Three years later in 1940, she enrolled in Nyack, graduating in 1942.

Bea met Clair Bixler and fell in love.

He had sung with a dance group in Pennsylvania and struggled with God's call upon his life.

Surrender finally came.

After his graduation in 1943 they were married.

She added the third 'B' to her name.

Pastorates followed in North Carolina, New York, New Jersey, Pennsylvania, Michigan and Indiana and so did four children; Betsy, William, J. Robert, and Barbara.

This dear pastor's wife was busy.

Inspiration for Bea's music came from sermons, poems, scripture or prayers.

The words focused on the "nuts and bolts of the Gospel."

Leading in worship was her gift.

Widowed in 1983, this primrose did not fold.

She continued.

In demand as a conference musician, she wrote theme songs, traveled and shared her love of God in music.

In 2003, I was invited to speak at the Smoky Mountain Women's Retreat in Asheville, North Carolina.

Bea was the conference worship leader.

Millie Harris, a soloist and voice teacher in Virginia Beach, was sitting next to me as we prepared to enjoy the mini-concert Bea was to perform.

We marveled at what we heard.

A woman climbing the upper range of her eighties was able to play the piano and sing in that trained alto voice, holding a high F while her hands flew across the keys with flourish and a familiar grace.

"Jesus left Heaven to die in my *Plaaaace.*" (That's the F)
What mercy, what love and what grace."

God's Word says, "...*Burst into jubilant song with music.*" (Note 6)

And that's exactly what she does!
God has promised a harvest of blessing to the faithful.

"...That you may gather in your grain, new wine and oil...."
Deuteronomy 11: 14b

New wine is blessing, making the heart glad.

God was glad with Bea.

She had been favored through the years with working with Corrie Ten Boom, author of *Hiding Place.* Noted trombonist Bill Pearce of Chicago and Tedd Smith, Billy Graham's pianist played her music, "*Life Is a Symphony*" and "*I Am Not Worthy.*"

She was honored as the distinguished alumnus of the year at Nyack College in 1986.

The Singspiration Company published entire editions of her numbers.

Many Bixler songs are printed in the "Favorites" series, especially numbers 4, 5 and 7.

Composer of over 300 songs, in her eighties, she is not done.

Describing this time of her life she says, "It has been a series of subtractions and additions...a gallbladder was subtracted, then cataracts...next they added lenses and a hearing aid, then a knee was subtracted and a joint added."

God nurtures flourishing faith.

"I will keep on carrying you. When you are old, I'll be there bearing you...
I've done it and will keep on doing it, carrying you on my back, saving you."
(Note 7)

Adversity diverts us.

Worship centers us.

The first time I met Bea it was many years ago at the Brown County
Women's Retreat in Nashville, Indiana.

I was invited to speak and Bea was the retreat musician and worship
leader.

Since I am also a soloist I always weave music into each teaching
session as an enhancement to the truths shared.

When I had finished my first session, Bea began to rehearse for the
evening.

She asked me to come over to the piano and look at the piece, *"I Am
Not Worthy"* and sing it.

I did.

Then she suggested I close out my second session in the evening with it.

I did.

A woman standing in the hallway had stumbled into our retreat and
sat down at a table in the back as I closed with singing, *"I Am Not
Worthy."*

She was not a part of the retreat, just a hotel guest.

Drawn by the words of hope she came into our meeting.

Just minutes before, a telephone call had come in and she was
summoned to the desk with the news that her husband had died
suddenly.

Broken in heart, new grief to bear, she desperately needed the message
of God's unconditional Love.

"I am not worthy the least of his favor but Jesus left Heaven for me...."

A seed faith choked by the weeds of neglect was unearthed that night and a prodigal came home.

It was Bea's music that pointed the way back.

Bea Bixler is a rare flower of resilience in God's garden.

"...Sing to the Lord a new song." (Note 8)

So she wrote, *"I Sing A New Song."*

And she sang it.

Songs of blessing poured out of her soul; *"If You Only Knew," "I Hear the Voice of Jesus," " Life is a Symphony," "The Prodigal's Prayer"* and so many others.

Her music tape *"All To The Glory of God"* is an offering revealing the heart of worship.

"Hear this...I will sing to the Lord, I will sing
...I will make music to the Lord." (Note 9)

And she did.

A Blessing Harvest is hers.

Into her eight decade, she continues with flourishing faith.

Autumn rain does its work.

Blessing is always raining down on God's committed.

What will we be doing in our eighth decade?

It is something to think about.

Will we continue to create and give when our bodies want us to stop?

Will our love of Jesus be brand new every morning?

"...Give yourselves completely to God...since you have been given a new life...Use your whole body as a tool for the glory of God." (Note 10)

One day while visiting her semi-invalid mother, she was washing clothes downstairs in a worn out washer that kept spewing water everywhere. The four children were upstairs romping, as kids do. Thinking about her mother's illness and all that surrounded her, she suddenly felt comfort. The Lord was near. When the water stopped, words of praise came to her.

"In the midst of trouble, He hears me,
In the midst of trouble, He cheers me,
I seek His face and I ask for grace
In the hardest place
As I run the race;
Though the sky is dark above me,
I am sure He'll always love me.
The heaviest burden He always shares.
In the midst of trouble He cares."

His comfort is never far away from Bea.
He is always close to us.

Her favorite song, *"It May Be Today"* was also her mother's.

Inspiration came while doing dishes and thinking about life. Off to the tired old church piano she went and penned the words, putting it to music.

> *"The Christ I love is coming soon.*
> *It may be morning, night or noon.*
> *My lamp is lit,*
> *I'll watch and pray.*
> *It may be today—It may be today."*

Anticipating Heaven is a part of the Harvest of faith.

Bea is still blooming for Jesus,
Truly, a pristine one of a kind primrose.
And Heaven looks down and smiles.

PONDER POINT:

- Have I used my talent and gifts for God's Glory?
- Have I hoarded what I have for my own benefit?
- Will I believe God is able to grow my faith and make it flourish into my eighties?

PRAYER POINT:

Wonderful Jesus;

Author and finisher of my faith,

What have I done with the seeds of my life?

Have I trusted YOU to grow them or did I bury them in a place where they were dug up by the world's promise.

I know YOU have created me for your pleasure and that my response to you is worship.

What have I worshipped other than YOU?

I want YOUR PLAN, YOUR LIFE to blossom in me.

Forgive me.

Love me.

Use me.

FOR YOUR GLORY, I exist.

Take my life and let it be consecrated unto Thee.

11

Harvest Bounty

Faith needs witness.

Bounty is reward.

We all want it.

Industrious gardeners know that trees are the prized treasure of the garden. They are the focus around which design is created.

They must also be nurtured, pruned, fed and watered.

A thorough autumn rain always provides the deep moisture to the roots of established trees preparing them for winter and disaster if it strikes.

Unfortunately, we gardeners tend to take the beauty of the tree for granted, neglecting the proper care until something happens and then it is a last ditch effort to save it.

In July 2003, something did happen in our town.

A freak, straight-line wind blew through at 85 mile per hour winds.

Overnight, hundreds of trees were leveled. There were 350,000 people without power, some for long as three weeks.

The earth was dug up and we were undone.

Downtown, a construction crane was leaning precariously against a tall building, rendering it unsafe and for several days engineers studied the best way to take it down. The building was evacuated. At intersections, traffic lights dangled and swung dangerously close to the automobiles attempting escape, as telephone poles bent almost in half seemed to bow down to the havoc of the storm.

In the midtown section of our city where renovation is on going to restore historic homes, chaos was evident. The finely settled oaks, maples, pears and dogwoods were gone. Many fell through the center of some of these homes.

Every place we looked, trees were gone.

On our street it was our pear trees.

My mother lost three and we lost limbs off two.

One was strategically placed in my backyard English garden.

It was the corner I loved the most.

Providing lush foliage, the graceful arms seemed to hover and shelter the numerous autumn fern underneath and the myriad of delicate azaleas in pastel colors of lavender and pink. Angel statuary rests against its trunk like an ongoing prayer.

Now one of the massive limbs is gone, severed as it crashed through the fence tearing a hole.

It will never be the same.

A wounded tree.

Clean up began immediately, continuing for weeks and then months.

The sounds of buzz saws could be heard in every neighborhood as the limbs of felled trees were sawed, chopped, stacked and made ready to be hauled away.

Laboring long into the humid, summer heat, people reached out and tried to help one another in every way possible.

Storms seem to reduce us as well by revealing what we can live without.

Clutter took charge of our streets.

Stacks of wood continued to pile up until houses were obscured.

It took most of the summer to get rid of the mess.

Deadwood lying around.

Six months later, after going through the fall and winter, our nurseryman came out to survey our garden areas to see what needed to be done.

By now, we could analyze what had really made it through the storm. A new look at refurbishing the beds was necessary for the sun and shade ratio had significantly been rearranged from the tree damage. Upon investigating the two trees, gaping holes had been ripped into the sides. Trunks were exposed to the elements. The one in the front had begun to heal itself according to our nurseryman's expertise.

I had never thought about a tree healing itself.

The tree in back had lost an arm but the gash was not as noticeable as the front tree. Our nurseryman, Trip said, "Leave them as they are. Don't take them down. Just watch and wait."

Autumn rains had come and gone as well as the piercing of freezing temperatures and they both stood as a witness, surviving the severe and sudden storm.

Trees define the horizon,

Bearers of Beauty,

Bounty for a gardener's heart.

They provide relief from the starkness of unending space.

They nurture life, caring for what they protect.

They stand as a witness,

And so must we.

There is a striking silhouette of a man walking the line with his feet firmly planted on earth but his head looking toward the heavens. His profile is bold and rugged. Wherever his path has taken him, his image is recognizable, a magnanimous shadow against the sky's full expanse.

An exposed life;

An indomitable faith.

Faith found in the cotton fields of Arkansas.

Faith sung about at the knee of his mother, Carrie, as she picked a guitar and gathered her children together after a hard day's work.

Faith to believe that you can dream and God will hear you.

Faith to hold on to, when his much loved fourteen-year-old brother Jack was at the point of death from a serious school shop accident, and yet even Jack held on until Papa Cash got there.

Faith to go on when Jack entered heaven and he was left here to continue without Jack.

Faith matters to God and so did this man's future.

"Let your roots grow down into Christ

And draw up nourishment from him.

See that you go on growing in the Lord and become strong and vigorous in the truth." (Note 1)

J.R. Cash, which is his given name and is what family members called him until he became famous, was this man.

Affectionately we have called him John, but never Johnny.

He had big faith and it stood out like a lone oak tree against the horizon.

It stood as a witness.

The tree had weathered storms, famine, drought, snow, and floods and there were marks on it to prove what it had endured.

Johnny Cash is known the world over as a country music legend.

A troubadour, storyteller, writer, he defied being categorized or labeled.

When he would say, "Hello, I'm Johnny Cash," the world would open its arms and receive his gift.

Books will be written about his music, the ups and downs of his life, and the impact on the generations of people who enjoyed his style but his faith tells the tale.

The witness of a life so rooted in faith has its own unique flourishing beauty.

It stands alone in a world where the colors run together and there is little clarity.

The man in black became a symbol of perseverance.

Heaven and Hell battled for him.

His wounds were apparent but so was his faith.

This was not ambiguous faith but clear-cut Christian faith found in Jesus Christ.

Real faith finds a way to grow.

When my husband Roy and I married in 1963, we did not have an automobile.

He was in flight training in Pensacola, Florida.

The beginning gross pay for a new Ensign in the US Navy was $222.20 a month.

My parents came to visit us and we decided to go car shopping.

We needed a car.

Managing to find a little Plymouth Valiant, which would meet our needs, was great but we still had to come up with about $300.00 to make the deal work. Some royalty money for the song, *I Still Miss Someone*" was coming in the fall. Roy and John are co-authors of this music. Praying about it one evening and not wanting to ask either set of our parents for the loan, Roy asked John, his uncle, to loan us this amount.

A few days later a check arrived.

When we got our royalty check in November, we sent the $300.00 back to John with a note thanking him for helping us out in a pinch.

Do you ever forget folks who do that?

Families have needs.

God provides.

A heart cared.

Another example comes to mind of John's interest in others.

My husband had a Martin guitar.

It was stolen in a move from the east coast to the west coast.

Sentimental, valuable, irreplaceable.

John responded.

He gave one of his to Roy.

A heart that gave.

The following years of Navy life brought us together at concerts along the way.

John and June came to Newport, RI in 1975 while Roy was at the Naval War College and did a free concert for the military families.

All four services were represented as well as many foreign countries.

It was an evening of laughter, tears, trains and the American Flag.

Visiting Harvard professors were screaming and stomping their feet to the Cash rhythms.

His music crossed all boundaries.

Always when we got together with them as families, the talk was about faith not music.

Faith needs refortifying.

Sharing sharpens perspective.

Real faith reaches towards real faith.

On the road, at home, in a church,

In a seeking heart.

In his autobiography entitled *Cash*, he reveals how his faith became rooted.

It was the window to his life.

John loved to perform.

Traveling in his specially configured tour bus brought pleasure.

He looked forward to going to the plantation in Jamaica for rest.

Recharging his spirit took place at Bon Aqua, his farm.

All of his homes, he thoroughly enjoyed.

Children grew up, married and reproduced.

The tremendous insight of John's spiritual renewal is that it was going on all the time. When he would retreat to Bon Aqua, there was a garden he worked. Books of theology, literature, and poetry were placed there for him to peruse, as well as his Bible.

The writer's soul was fed.

The poet relished beauty.

The philosopher pondered.

The gardener worked out life by working in the earth.

There was a hunger for spiritual truth that led both him and June into a Bible correspondence study program. When he graduated he said, "...The experience was both exciting and humbling. I learned just enough to understand that I knew almost nothing." (Note 2)

Spoken in true Cash form.

He would cut to the chase with truth.

Solitude, thinking, writing, common work in the soil were the things that made his life ready to go on the road again.

He loved weather.

"Sitting in my library looking out the westward-facing window at the strengthening rain and the blackening sky above the deep green fields of this beautiful place...I feel good...secure...short of a tornado, nothing can hurt me here...it's an intimate feeling, safe and snug...different from the anticipation of the storm. That's more exciting: exhilarating because I know it'll be such a big and glorious show...huge forces...touching the lives of...men, plants...creatures and on a small scale...the tiny personal universe inside me...For me such moments are open invitations to closeness with God. Nature at work isn't itself God, but it is evidence of Him and by letting myself be drawn into its depths and intrigues, I can come to Him: see the glory of His creation, feel the salve of His grace." (Note 3)

Now I know why I have always loved storms.

They do reveal God.

John's life was filled with them.

Broken relationships, addictive reality, troubled friends, exploitation, family crises,

But His God was always present in the storm with him.

He drew comfort and strength from that knowledge.

It made him secure, safe, held.

"If you abide in my word, then you are truly disciples of Mine." (Note 4)

He loved God's Word.

He knew when he was abiding and when he was not.

A transparent faith allows you to look inside.

It is a witness.

When 2003 entered the calendar of our lives we did not anticipate three Cash funerals in a marching succession from March to September.

Aunt Louise, the oldest sister of John's was the first, followed by June's in May and John's in September.

The faith of their lives was bountifully on display in death.

In fact, it was profoundly prominent.

Rosanne Cash paid one of the most moving tributes I have ever heard at a funeral—to June, her stepmother.

Ironically it was about not using the word "step" in their family for when John and June married that was a distinction they made.

There would be no stepparents and no stepchildren.

They would be family.

She recounted a humorous story revealing June's caring personality with people.

A telephone call came in one day. Rosanne realized that June had been on the phone for about thirty minutes. When she got off, Rosanne asked her about the phone call. June begin communicating how many children the woman had, what her life was about and what she was doing on that day. To which, Rosanne said, "She must be a close friend." June replied, " No, it was a wrong number."

We laughed but we got a clear snapshot of a true people person.

A heart that cared.

Jane Seymour, English actress and star of the Dr. Quinn television series, spoke about the kind of friend June was, how she cared enough to share with her the love of Jesus.

A heart that witnessed.

Rosanne Cash was the one chosen to eulogize June.

We heard of June's love for flowers, gardens, big hats, children and grandchildren.

She told us that June affirmed every child in the family, encouraging them.

A heart that edified.

A poignant memory captured her grief and was a tribute of June's love.

It was to be a special birthday party planned by John for June and all the grandchildren were coming to Virginia. They were going to canoe down the river to a designated landing, get out and picnic in the beautiful outdoors.

June had Virginia roots.

She loved the country.

A perfect day of beauty was planned.

She decided to go ahead of the children in order to be standing at the dock to welcome them when they arrived.

When they saw her they must have screamed with delight.

There she was, wearing one of her long flowing dresses and a favorite floppy garden hat, silk scarf in hand.

What a moment.

As the children came insight, June hollered,

"Yoo Hoo! I've been waiting for you."

Smiles, laughter, hug and kisses followed and a wonderful time of togetherness was created.

What a day to tuck away in thought like a lovely summer painting.

Rosanne, emotional and tender, alluded to Heaven when she said, "And one day when we cross that river, she'll be standing there on the shore waving her silk scarf and saying, "Yoo Hoo! I've been waiting for you."

We were moved to tears by this sensitive tribute of love disclosing the reality of June's faith.

A faith so lived that her children could envision her in heaven, waiting for them.

There were many words that brought honor to June's life.

An ill, debilitated, grieving husband, who was brought to the funeral in a wheelchair, stood up and bid an earthly farewell to his bride of thirty-six years.

The presence of God seemed to gently fall upon us as we joined in singing the old hymn *"Farther Along"* and minutes later, we were.

In September we assembled again as a family.

This time it was to mourn and celebrate the life of John.

It had been four wrenching months since June's death.

He had lost his soul mate.

God performed a good work in John's life—He not only started it, He finished it.

"I am sure that God who began a good work within you will keep right on helping you grow in his grace until his task within is finished…" (Note 5)

Friends, famous and infamous, shared their heart about a man who gave his freely.

Stories surfaced sharing the bounty of his life.

Seeing a one-legged stranger on the side of a road, he stopped the car and inquired.

Within days the man was fitted with a prosthesis and was able to walk.

Kris Kristofferson, with tears streaming down his face, told of being a janitor at Colombia records waiting for a break.

John and June reached out to him and he got it.

Kris turned directly to the audience and interjected, "And if you don't have Jesus, you ain't got nothing."

Kristofferson's music was discovered and Jesus was part of the transaction.

Larry Gatlin spoke movingly about a time when money was short and rent was overdue.

John paid it for two months enabling him to have a home for his family.

An orphanage in Jamaica benefited.

Pastors shared intimate relationships with him.

Testimonies of charity, grace, love, and friendship flowed one heart to another.

There was grief with hope and grief with no hope present on that day among the mourners.

The difference is found in faith.

Faith in Jesus.

Days before John went to Heaven he was thinking and studying about it.

Tom Cash, his younger brother, told us this story: I walked in to see J.R. and he was holding the Bible. I asked him what he was reading and he said, "I'm studying Matthew 24." "What are you learning?" Tom asked. John said, "I am learning about the second coming of Christ." "What do you think about it?" his brother asked.

He said, "I can't wait."

How ironic that his last release was entitled *"When The Man Comes Around."*

Indeed, he had been thinking about this message.

His sister, Jo Anne related her story:

She and her husband Harry are in ministry in a church in Nashville.

When she went to John's home to take a turn sitting with her brother a few days before he died, he asked her a question. He said, "Jo Anne, if you were going to meet Jesus, what do you think He would say to you?" She responded, "Well, I'm not sure, John."

He then said, "I think He would say to you, feed my sheep."

A dying man who was studying his Bible, looking forward to meeting Jesus, encouraging his sister to continue in ministry, is not a man without hope.

His soul was ready to soar.

What witness.

What bounty.

The music video *"Hurt"* speaks to the significance of his achievements from his perspective of a life closing on earth.

Penetrating words,

Alluding to an empire turned to dirt,

Wounds that make us hurt,

Faith that carries us through.

Faith in Jesus.

The image of the Cross flashes through this video revealing his family through the years;

We see his mother, Carrie, wife June, and his children.

Their importance unfolds with photographs of the past; moments lived in a whirlwind's breath.

It truly was a testament of faith left behind…

On purpose.

Sometimes John spelled it out along the way.

When questioned about why he would go to Las Vegas and perform, he would respond with the words the Pharisees used about Jesus, "*He dines with publicans and sinners.*" (Note 6)

The apostle Paul said, "*I have become all things to all men that by all possible means I might save some.*" (Note 7)

That was the quality that drew people. Fearlessly and without apology he could go anywhere to perform because he knew whom he was. He was a witness.

In describing himself, he said, "I don't have Paul's calling—but sometimes I can be a signpost. Sometimes I can sow a seed. And post hole diggers and seed sowers are mighty important in the building of the Kingdom." (Note 8)

Those that love God continue to gather in a harvest.

"That you may gather in grain, new wine and oil…." Deuteronomy 11: 14b

In November 2003, after his death, we were in Branson, Missouri and attended Larry Gatlin's Christmas Show.

He paid tribute to both John and June by showing a film clip of them singing together, obviously done just months before they died.

We had never seen it.

John talks about their "bodies wearing down and not workin' so good." Then he says, "When we get to feelin' so bad physically, we just sing about Heaven and get better."

I do not remember the song.

What I remember is the sight of these two old fragile faces singing about Heaven and when they had finished he turned to her and said, "Now Honey, don't you feel better?"

She said, "Yes, I sure do, John."

The oil of gladness was upon their faces.

The beauty of faith was seen.

A Harvest of faith was theirs.

They were ready.

What bounty.

What witness.

"Dostoyevsky's essential love of life and joy in all God's creation found a surer expression…. Beauty is not only a terrible thing, it is a mysterious thing. There, God and the Devil strive for mastery and the battleground is the heart of men." (Note 9)

The "Man in Black" wore black for the cares of the world. He took up His cross and followed hard after God.

The Cross transformed him.

The root of faith begins and grows a living tree entrenched and stable in the midst of devastation.

A deliberately defined faith characterized his music and life.

He wrote and sang about it.

Experienced and lived it.

As a Cash fan, you'll have to deal with it because its influence was alive.

Once again we see a silhouette. A silhouette of a man dressed in a long black coat with a guitar held close to his side, standing like a lone oak tree. A robust, craggy uncompromising oak reaching up to the heavens.

His face, like flint, is focused up in anticipation—anticipation reaching to the heavens, and spanning out across the earth as a witness. Where his music has gone, his faith will go along with it.

This is the portrait of a man the world will not soon forget.

PONDER POINT:

- Why does the word "witness" intimidate people?
- What effect does reading a life story like this have on you?
- Will your faith be remembered when your life is over?

PRAYER POINT:

Beloved Father;
How much YOU have loved me and how quickly the seasons pass before me.
Have I been a witness to those around me?
Can I be a witness wherever YOU send me?
Lord, give me a desire to be a witness for YOU.
Heaven is waiting.
Maybe that's it.
I have forgotten my destination.
Remind me every day.
Help me care about bringing someone along with me.
Keep me working, praying, believing and proclaiming YOU.

I want my faith to stand as a mighty oak with a solid belief in the Word of God.
I want my worship to be fragrant with love abounding for others.
I want to be your witness.

Follow

Follow the Christ, the King!
Live pure.
Speak true.
Right wrong.
Follow the Else wherefore born!
Alfred Lord Tennyson

Transforming the Landscape

Faith changes everything.

The barren earth begs for beauty.
Landscapes need design.

It was our first home and we were excited.
Room to grow.
A new section of Rancho Bernardo community was being developed for young families like us.
Contracting people were out every day, building.
San Diego, California was affordable in the 1970's.
Kellye would be in first grade and her school, Westwood, was just a few blocks away.
It never occurred to us that when we bought the house, we would not "get a yard."
In the south when a new area is being designed, grass and bushes are usually thrown in and one might even have a couple of trees.
Grass, for sure, was a given.
Not so this time.
We loved the house but we had to have a landscaping design.

The front needed to be low maintenance but I still wanted growing plants, not rocks.

A play area was very important for the back.

Beauty, green, flowering, described what we desired; and a few trees would be nice.

The front became a bed of English ivy and we had a Magnolia tree planted as a touch of "home."

The back became a circular swirl of grass bordered by daisies and gazanias.

A Willow tree was the centerpiece of the back.

Everything revolved around it.

The extreme right side yard had a sand area for a swing set in which a rowdy little boy could play to his heart's content.

I had one so I knew what I needed.

And the plan worked.

The Magnolia tree was my southern root.

The English Ivy reflected my love for a country for which I had always held a fascination.

The grass was practical.

The daises and gazanias fed me beauty.

The sand lot was for real life with kids.

The landscaping plan really did transform the bare earth.

Functional beauty.

Looking back I can now see how God was laying out a design for me.

A plan of transformation,

I was a caterpillar in my own garden.

The caterpillar life is slow, low and easily smashed.

Purpose was not a priority.

Existing was.

A daily, predictable, familiar struggle.

Getting through.

The caterpillar ambles along to somewhere, to do something of which he's not sure.

If he does not take a risk and learn how to spin, he never becomes what he was intended to be—a new creature.

DIFFERENT

The cocoon phase is mammoth in importance because it is the internal process that must occur if the butterfly is to emerge as a gloriously winged creature, able to soar.

No one can shortcut the process and help the creature get out of the cocoon ahead of God's schedule for He orchestrates all of life, even the caterpillar's.

The creature inside that is becoming must find his own way out.

God participates, however, in this seemingly solo effort.

"Rejoice...the Lord is near." (Note 1)

"The earth is the Lord's and everything in it." (Note 2)

Even caterpillars.

The immense push in emerging from the cocoon is necessary to force the wings to be released correctly and thus be able to flap and then fly.

The wings must have pressure.

Once, a bystander actually took scissors and attempted to enlarge the opening of the mouth of the cocoon to aid the process.

It was a sad and dismal failure.

The swollen creature never became.

It stumbled around never realizing its purpose.

And so do we.

Butterflies go places that caterpillars will never go.

In fact, they draw nurture constantly from the many flowers provided along the way.

Provision.

God provides even for butterflies.

The landscape changes because of butterflies,

And...

We were created to transform the landscape.

At this time of my life, what was my present landscape?

An eleven-month Navy wartime deployment.

A husband in danger.

Children who needed security.

What did I feel?

Limitation,

Loneliness,

Listlessness,

Longing for more of God.

ME.

My purpose had to be found in Him; and I had to serve His purpose.

"...David...served the purpose of God in his own generation." (Note 3)

Bible study, prayer, fellowship, service—disciplines to grow.

In my weakness He stooped to give me purpose.

"Many are the plans in a man's heart but it is the Lord's purpose that prevails." (Note 4)

He will not let go of our lives until we find our purpose.

My idea of serving surrounded perfection.

Until now that idea had also had helped me escape.

Because no one is perfect, right?

So it was easy to eliminate myself.

Wrong.

God uses the weak, the imperfect.

Paul said, "I will boast all the more gladly about my weaknesses, so that Christ's power may rest on me...for when I am weak, then I am strong." (Note 5)

He "...understands every weakness of ours." (Note 6)

The Holy Spirit "…helps us in our weakness." (Note 7)

His power does the work so we must be weak,
But we have to know it.

This was the year of Relationship with my God.
The caterpillar had attention deficit syndrome.
Spiritual mindlessness.
How we wander away from what is relevant to God.
Because we wander away from God Himself.

We matter; others matter, because God matters.

Captive, overwhelmed, impoverished in our pathetic caterpillar lives, we discover purpose.
We were meant to fly, to bring His beauty to the world, to feed and nurture and grow the landscape, changing its borders and redefining the garden.

I knew my home was the starting point because your story begins there.
"Being precedes doing. What you do emerges from who you are." (Note 8)
Butterfly-like life has arrived. It has begun—it is radical. It takes a storehouse of faith to fly.
His promise to us is this: "**…I will provide…and you will eat and be satisfied." Deuteronomy 11: 15**

The landscape of the world is transformed through ordinary people.
I met Alba in the Dominican Republic in April 2003.
My hostess, Chita, had taken me to meet Alba, who was recovering from knee surgery.

It was obvious that Chita had a dear friendship with Alba. She and her husband Salvador attended the church with Chita and Frank, who serve as missionaries in Santo Domingo. We were welcomed into her charming bungalow. I noticed immediately, upon the walls of her home, a collection of eye-catching artwork, paintings. Alba was the artist herself, and the art was very good. Also, alongside the art was an exquisite portrait of Alba as a young woman in her twenties, movie star beautiful. She laughed when I told her that but indeed it was true.

Chita, who was proficient in Spanish, and I, who was not, now had the unique experience of communication with Alba.

With a smile on her face and a twinkle in her eye, Chita asked Alba to tell me her faith story.

Without hesitation she began to do so.

Chita was in the middle, interpreting to me, line upon line, phrase upon phrase, and (I might add) with animation.

Speak, listen, turn, look, interpret, smile and start over.

This was the process among three people, only one of whom completely understood the other two.

What a tenacious search for truth.

When Alba was a young girl, she loved to visit the home of her English aunt and spend wonderful moments with her. Loving to go to her home, she spent some wonderful times with her. After dinner, this aunt would always retire to her room with a little black book.

Alba was curious about the book.

She knew the aunt loved it.

When the aunt passed away some years later, the family asked Alba if there was anything she would like to have that belonged to the aunt.

She remembered the little black book.

Not knowing if she would recognize it, down to the home of the aunt she traveled.

After searching through many boxes, there it was.

Opening it, Alba saw the hand written notes that graced the pages and was thrilled to have it as her own.

But there was a problem now.

Alba did not know how to read and understand it.

Taking the little black book to a religious leader nearby, she asked him for help.

He discouraged her and asked her not to pursue this.

But Alba was determined.

She clung to it, wondering if she would ever know its contents.

Her family moved later on into a city area and there was a church across the street.

One Sunday morning, she opened the window to listen to the stirring music being sung.

It was an English speaking church and she, being Spanish, could not understand much, but she was strangely warmed, not knowing why.

Suddenly her heart was so full of longing; she cried out, "It's Jesus. It's Jesus that I need. Come, Jesus, come."

He came.

She became His child that day and the landscape changed again.

Alba learned to read and love the little black book.

It was the Bible.

Joy invaded her life and purpose bloomed.

A seed had been transplanted from an English aunt who knew and loved Jesus.

Alba's inquiring heart would not give up its search for Truth.

God heard her cry to Him and the seed of true faith was planted in her heart.

Such radiance transformed her countenance as she spoke her story to me in Spanish, and I actually understood her message with my heart even though I did not comprehend her words.

She began to follow Jesus, and through the years she has grown in her love, proclaiming Him.

Alba and Salvador are very active in their faith journey together but are still burdened for other family members who still do not know Jesus as their Savior.

I knew my appointment was to pray for these precious people, her family by name.

I prayed for her family.

She prayed for mine.

The God of all Gods heard us, each in our own language, as we became one voice in prayer unto Him.

When I said goodbye, we embraced and Alba gave me one of her paintings as a gift—a still life of fruit on a table, an inviting basket of strawberries and a white pitcher filled with golden flowers.

It is my Dominican treasure.

It will remind me of the landscape of Jesus' Love that is changing this island nation one person at a time.

We are all on a mission and God directs where we go and what we do.

I shall not forget what God did in one seeking heart that now exhibits flourishing faith, faith that will not quit.

Just recently I received an exciting e-mail from my friends, Chita and Frank, who told of another faith break-through in a local family.

A father and mother, Maggie and Miguel, have now received the gift of God's Love and because of their new seed faith, six children are watching.

For one year, Frank taught a Bible study every week, one to one, to this family.

Can you imagine the commitment to prepare every week for a year to teach one family?

Can you imagine a father and mother who would come with all their children week after week? Surely God will hear the prayers of these parents.

If we seek God we will find Him.

They did and the landscape changed once again, for the sowing of the Word reaps Faith.

Transplanted love seeds faith.

Nations come to know God one soul at a time.

A flourishing faith continues to gather in order to give away.

The provision of God is always there, always enough.

He makes a way.

"The strength and happiness of a man consists in finding out
the way in which God is going and going in that way too."
—Henry Ward Beecher

Chuck Colson found the way.

As the Watergate burglary stalked the Nixon White House, in 1974, a related charge associated to the obstruction of justice in the Daniel Ellsberg case was levied against Chuck Colson.

He pleaded guilty.

He was a significant part of the inner circle that surrounded the president.

A man of influence.

In 1974, entering Alabama's Maxwell prison as the first member of the Nixon administration to be incarcerated for Watergate-related charges, he also came to prison as a new Christian.

Dubbed "the hatchet man," he was feared by the weak and the strong in politics.

"When the news of Colson's conversion to Christianity leaked to the press in 1973, the Boston Globe reported, 'If Mr. Colson can repent of his sins, there just has to be hope for everybody.'" (Note 9)

And the good news is: They got it right.

Behind the closed bars of prison life, God Almighty began a new work in Chuck Colson's life.

Serving seven months out of a one-to-three year sentence, he could see that hope needed to be planted in the lives of prisoners.

Men need reconciliation.

Families of prisoners need assistance.

Churches need involvement.

To bring these concerns together in a viable way, Prison Fellowship Ministries was born in 1976.

Some scoffers thought Colson would get over his newfound religion, but he didn't.

It was not religion.

It was relationship.

Faith based relationship with the living God grows and reproduces itself.

Almost 25 years later, this dynamic outreach to prisoners, ex-prisoners and their families is networked through churches of all denominations.

It is the largest organization of its kind.

In 1979, Prison Fellowship International came into existence as a global endeavor to meet needs of prisoners and families abroad, and 88 countries are now a part of this ongoing effort.

In 1983, Justice Fellowship, a faith-based criminal justice reform group was established to provide dialogue between diverse philosophical viewpoints within the criminal justice system.

Angel Tree, a program existing under Prison Fellowship Ministries, was launched to provide Christmas presents and Christian summer camp experiences for the children of prisoners.

Colson, author of twenty books, gives all his royalties back into the funding of Prison Fellowship.

Recipient of various honorary degrees and awards, Mr. Colson was also awarded the one million dollar Templeton Prize for Progress in Religion in 1993, which was donated to Prison Fellowship.

A man's heart found its purpose in serving the God who changed his heart.

The landscape of prison life has been transformed with purpose, promise and personal growth.

God provides.

In my own city of Memphis, I had an opportunity to go this year into the Mark Luttrell Correctional Center as a guest speaker for women.

Bible studies have been going on for almost three years with women from my church. Just being with them the first time, it was obvious what God was planting in the lives of the prisoners.

God's Love was growing.

Compassion was shared.

Perseverance was rooted.

Faith was flourishing.

Pam and Judy are the leaders, teaching in Bible studies.

Gathering a faithful group of women to join them, they all come and minister every week, building friendships, praying and loving the prisoners who love them back.

I witnessed this exchange.

It was such a joy to see God's Love demonstrated with such sincerity and integrity.

One autumn day last year, a prisoner named Regina was greatly disappointed because a parole board had turned her down.

She felt God had abandoned her.

Having been a Christian for a couple of years, she just knew He was going to help her get out.

Her request had been denied.

Prayer went out for Regina.

Prayer opens the way for us to hear from God.

Sometimes we are buried in circumstance.

Regina was.

As I prayed for her, I also felt she needed a book, my book, *Light Breaking Through.*

It is about trusting God's timing.

Pam came to my home, picked it up and gave it to her.

Several weeks letter I received an affirming letter encompassing every chapter of the book. She shared how God had encouraged her, but the most startling piece was about the cover. Regina said, "What kind of woman sends you a book on God's timing when He's rejected you? I did not want to read this book. I was angry and could not read my Bible either, but I kept coming back to the cover again and again."

Obviously I knew what was on the cover.

It is a clump of pine trees with God's light breaking through.

What else did she see?

She continued, "Finally I saw what He wanted me to see. In the right-hand corner in the background is a small cross. When all else is removed, there is still the cross."

That was the message she received.

I ran and picked up the book, perused the cover and there it was.

I had this book in my possession for over a year and had never seen the small, obscure but defined cross in the right-hand corner of the cover of my book.

I had not seen the CROSS.

It was there all the time.

It always is.

A prisoner, feeling hopeless and defeated, had discovered the CROSS, again.

The night I met her, she did not know I was coming to speak.

In she walked into Bible study carrying her Bible and my book, *Light Breaking Through*.

She was very excited when she discovered that I was there and we hugged.

All around me were faces reflecting their hearts.

Some were eager, hungry hearts.

Some were sad and despondent, but Christ was in our midst.

We had moments of laughter and moments of strong truth and both were received.

Regina beamed with God's Love.

Why?

Because His Love had been brought into prison faithfully by His own who cared and responded to the call to serve.

I was changed.

I prayed, "Help me, oh God, to write and proclaim Your Love to all You send. Send me. Thank you for using my book."

I saw the captive set free that night.

What a work of grace.

Beauty is growing behind those walls and there is flourishing faith that will make a difference outside where children and family members are growing.

The landscape is changing because of the seed of love growing in hearts now captive to God.

"Transforming faith happens…only in the context of movement. The power of God comes to those who obey…obedience means taking action—to love one another, to restore a relationship…God promises to give us power as we act." (Note 10)

We must act on what we know to do.

Joshua was chosen to obey and lead.

And so are we.

In Chapter three of the book of Joshua, a dilemma is presented.

Joshua has been instructed to march toward the border of Canaan; the Promised Land so long eluded by the wandering children of Israel.

We wander too.

They are to go and occupy.

And so are we.

A river at flood stage was the problem.

There will always be a flood of uncertainties and fears to face as we go.

How could they get across?

How will we?

"The command comes from God to Joshua to organize the people in a straight line behind the Ark of the Covenant and march directly toward the raging waters in a beeline to Canaan. The promise is this: Somewhere along the way God will intervene…Israel must take the first steps of faith…it is only when the people in the front line had actually entered the river that God miraculously parted the waters." (Note 11)

And we must take the first step to serve.

God's design for our lives is to follow Him and change the landscape.

A harvest of faith brings abundance.

"Live as if you were to die tomorrow."
Isadore of Seville

Then you will live abundantly.
The autumn rain does its work.
As we obey, He provides.

"Apart from me you can do nothing." (Note 12)

Together we will transform the landscape.

Faith can bloom behind prison walls.
It can bloom in impossibility.
It can bloom forever and set us free.

Regina, now free from prison, is sowing seeds of faith in her own garden.

PONDER POINT:

- What will change if I serve God?
- Can I trust His timing?
- Will I live as a caterpillar or a butterfly the rest of my life?
- Will I leave my comfort zone to serve another?

PRAYER POINT:

Sovereign Lord,
YOU know me.
My caterpillar's heart is trembling with risk.
If I follow YOU will YOU be there at every turn?
Apart from You I am nothing; therefore, I can do nothing.
But believing that YOU have used my whole life to prepare me to serve You,
I surrender again.
Even the part I have kept for myself.
This is new territory for me.
Something has grown in my garden, slowly, deliberately.
It is devotion.
It has choked out duty that had little beauty.
Let it flower, Oh God, every day.
Feed, nurture and prune it from other entanglements.
Allow it to become so dominant that only YOU are seen.
I will serve YOU and the landscape will change.
Thank You for running after me to make me into something beautiful.
I will follow You.

13

Bumper Crop Harvest

Faith leaves a legacy.

A garden needs birdsong.

Birds echo the coming season.

Sometimes they also bring seed, nonchalantly dropping it into the earth as they wing a flight overhead from somewhere remote.

God has surprises for us.

He plans them.

One such brisk autumn day, I spied a new struggling, spindly shoot attempting birth.

I did not recall planting anything in that spot so I watched it come forth.

Little by little as the autumn rain came, it grew.

It was the gift of a burnished golden mum tinged with copper.

Transplanted into my garden.

The birds did it.

But God orchestrated.

I never see a mum that I do not think about high school cheerleading and football games.

We cheerleaders always wore mums as corsages.

They seemed to be hardy enough to take the wear and tear of screaming, jumping, hugging, laughing teens.

When the game was over, win or lose the mum survived.

Consequently they were dried and pressed into lots of scrapbooks.

They are also the bearers of autumn, a signal that change is coming.

I cannot control change.

I must live with it.

I cannot ignore it.

I must embrace it.

God is preparing us to labor in His harvest.

At harvest time, satisfaction has bloomed.

The basket spills over and is laden with deliciously ripened fruit.

We want our lives to have an enriched reaping.

We shall if we have worked the work of Him who sent us.

Transparent faith, rich in texture, rooted in Christ Jesus.

Root reveals Relationship.

Our time of leading is shorter than we think.

"It all goes by so fast...Oh earth, you're too wonderful
for anybody to realize you.... Do human beings ever
realize life while they live—every, every minute?"
Thornton Wilder, *Our Town*

No, we do not.

God knows He must call us to purpose.

That's what He does.

Our part is to choose to respond.

We will not finish the work.

Others behind us, prepared to take our place will continue it.

They will move into fields that have been plowed with Godly desire, not duty, willingly, not wantonly, and sown in expectancy and love with a harvest in mind.

We are not done yet.

Our investment is in readying others for leadership in the garden of faith.

They have promises to plant as we have done.

God will tend to them as He has to us.

The mentoring process is constantly at work in the life of the believer.

Someone is leading.

Someone is following.

Someone is ahead.

Someone is behind.

Occasionally we become aware of this process because someone tells us.

An e-mail came to my husband last year in late summer.

It was a stark reminder of those who watch those who lead.

This story is a bumper crop blessing, abundance brimming over *"like precious oil running down on Aaron's beard.* (Note 1)

It came from a young man named Robb.

He served on the USS El Paso, when my husband Roy was the commanding officer.

A reunion is planned in 2004 in Philadelphia to reconnect with all those who were a part of the ship's family at any time in service life.

Here is what Robb said:

> Sir:
>
> I was stationed onboard the El Paso from 1982-1986 and remember when you reported aboard as the Commanding Officer. Some of the best times of my life was when I was onboard that ship.

You never knew this but you had a huge impact on my life.

I had joined the navy after dropping out of the eleventh grade. The El Paso was my first tour of duty and I did the typical young sailor thing; drink, pass out, work, drink and pass out. One time while overseas when we were in port somewhere in France, I had too much to drink, came back to the boat and, after finding my rack...decided to take my stuffed animal Garfield and walk to the bridge wearing my Garfield boxers.

You were sitting in the Captain's chair enjoying the night sky and the lights of the city. We talked a bit and someone escorted me back to bed...that was the end of it.

Instead of finding myself standing in front of you explaining my actions, nothing happened except for a few words from my Operations boss.

I guess what I am trying to say is that while on onboard, you were not only the Captain of the El Paso but to many you were a father figure that many of us who didn't have.

Over the years I have thought of you, your kindness toward the crew...the way you treated all of us. I had Commanding officers before and after you that treated the crew like [dirt] and made life hard on us. We were underway a lot, but you always made each underway period, fun and interesting. You stand out in my mind not because of one thing you said but because of your attitude and actions.... After leaving the El Paso, I gave up drinking, moved up the ranks and due to some medical problems left the navy in late 1993 as a first class chief petty officer.

I went to school and am now a charge nurse in a hospital in Minnesota, enjoying life.

I had a son 6 days after leaving the El Paso and have raised him on my own since then. He will be 17 in August and is looking at the military as a stepping-stone…mainly due to the positive time I had in the navy.

I realize that none of this probably makes sense to you.

I have trouble putting into words what it was or what you did that turned me around. I just know that over the years whenever I look back or try to figure out what it was that did, your name comes up.

You took care of us guys in ways no other Commanding Officer could match.

I really feel I owe in no small part, my success as a father and as a man to your leadership, compassion and guidance.

You will probably never know just how many people looked up to you not only as Captain but also as a father…many of us didn't come from the best of families…fathers were absent in young lives.

You were one of a kind and will never be forgotten.

From the bottom of my heart, I thank you and thank God for bringing you into my life if only for a brief moment of time. In a large way, you were a Hero to me.

I am where I am today because of you.

I look forward to shaking your hand at the reunion in 2004.

With the utmost respect,

Robb S.
OSI (SW)

With tears flowing I read the heart of this young man.

We will not always know what others perceive.

When God places a Christian in leadership, He expects him to lead with integrity and honor, to care for those in his charge.

There will be fruit.

Flourishing faith is fed with the good things of God.

Satisfaction is choice fruit.

He *"redeems your life from the pit and crowns you with love and compassion…satisfies your desires with good things. "* (Note 2)

He gives us His Word.

He calls us to serve Him.

Some one is watching us today and somewhere the landscape is changing because a leader is responsible unto God.

A garden must be tended.

Beauty grows from surrender.

Surrender grows everything else.

As the old hymn reminds us:

Wherever He leads I'll go
I'll follow my Christ who loves me so
Wherever He leads I'll go.

We follow by loving and serving.

A satisfied life will be ours.

It is the promise to us from God's word.

Obeying, loving and serving bring provision.

"I will provide…and you will eat and be satisfied." Deuteronomy 11: 15

The flower of contentment begins to grow.

It has taken root even though we were not aware.

"I have learned the secret of contentment...whether in plenty or want...I can do all things through him who gives me strength" (Note 3)

Have learned is the key.

It is the process of growing satisfaction spiritually.

Your will not mine, Lord.

Your way not mine.

Your purpose becomes mine.

Contentment blooms.

Planting God's Love and growing satisfaction has continued through generations and will do so through ours.

What God purposes will grow and reproduce again and again.

It was the summer of 2003 when I heard about Rachel.

An urgent prayer alert went out for her life from a friend of mine.

While life guarding, she was struck by lightning. The seconds lost in the flow of oxygen to the brain left her in a coma with a grim prognosis.

Prayer began.

The constant faith of her family grew a grace that is unmeasured in today's world.

Rachel, an exuberant and lovely young college student, a runner, a lover of God was incapacitated, shut down, hanging on.

Her life had already had tremendous impact.

God called out intercessors all over this nation to pray for His healing in Rachel's life.

I am one of them.

In the past few months, Rachel has come out of the coma.

Movement is coming in leaps and bounds,

Eyes are moving to commands.

Swallowing freely is almost there.

Response to music and speech are at the threshold.

A fully equipped van has been provided to transport her.

People are volunteering to aid the family in her round-the-clock care.

Bills are being paid.

We believe God for a harvest in this life.

Crisis praying is now mission praying.

We are being changed.

Faith is being planted in hearts as God unfolds miracle after miracle.

Some are small victories but they are growing large abundant faith.

People are praying for Rachel.

She is growing.

I was so moved when I went to her web site one day and found this update from her father Steve.

He quoted the words of this familiar hymn and their flourishing faith revealed it.

Be Still My Soul

Be still my soul for God is on our side
Bear patiently the cross of grief or pain
Leave to thy God to order and provide
In every change He faithful will remain…

Be still my soul thy God doth undertake
To guide the future as He has the past
Thy hope, thy confidence let nothing shake;
All now mysterious shall be bright at last…

He then said this, "Our hope and confidence are fixed on Him. He is ordering and providing. He forever remains faithful. He is honored and pleased when we submit to His ways in grace and love. Would you honor and please Him today with me?

Pray on!"

Contentment is growing in the midst of their garden of faith.

Weeds of worry try to suffocate but the root is secure.

Yes, their garden has been ravaged but is being restored daily, moment-by-moment.

A bumper crop is coming for the Wade family.

"Blessed are those who trust in the Lord

They are like trees planted along a riverbank with roots that reach deep into the water.

Such trees are not bothered by the heat or worried by long months of drought

Their leaves stay green and they go right on producing delicious fruit." (Note 4)

When God is in the midst of impossibility, faith grows.

Her name is Julia.

She is from the country of Liberia.

An active member of a Bible class that my friend Peggy teaches, her praise songs bring delight to God and to the group, even though they do not understand her native language.

How?

God's love shines through her as she sings.

A vibrant Christian, widowed and mother of ten children, she has lived with a son and his family for the past three years in Virginia.

An anguished heart has wept and cried out to God daily for the needs of her children left behind in Liberia.

Food, shelter, medical attention are real concerns.

Monies collected and donated have been sent to her children by this class.

Her English is very broken but her faith is not.

It flows freely and meets you.

The first time I met her was at a conference for women.

I closed the afternoon session by singing the words to *"Beulah Land,"* reminding the women of Heaven.

> *Beulah Land I'm longing for you*
> *And some day on Thee I'll stand*
> *There my home shall be eternal*
> *Beulah Land Sweet Beulah Land*

When I started to sing, I became keenly aware of another voice singing with me.

I was standing on a platform at the podium.

This voice was somewhere in the room.

The voice did not know the words but somehow knew the meaning for there was empathy.

Every note was a complement as the rich soulful alto voice harmonized with my soprano.

Amazingly, the breath control, phrasing, rhythm were exact and in sync with me.

For a moment I could not imagine what was happening.

No words were audible but the sounds, in perfect pitch, were with me.

I wondered if I had a heavenly visitor.

I saw no one singing but someone was.

The next day after the conference was a Sunday.

At Peggy's Bible class, I discovered who it was.

It was Julia.

Her speech is difficult to comprehend but her faith is easily received.

It is a faith so planted in the satisfaction of God that contentment unfolds in her smile.

We were asked to stand and "sing together" the hymn before this caring group whom she has grown to love.

Once again, sounds—not words, humming—not phonetics, blended into praise unto the Creator.

Our audience was weeping.

We were rejoicing.

We were all one.

Julia turned to me and slowly, deliberately she spoke, *"Billeeeee,* one-day-we-shall-stand-together-on-the-shores-of-Beulah-Land-and-we-shall-have-no-problem-with-words."

Mentored by this group of women.

Julia had changed the landscape with God's Love and these women had changed the landscape of the nation of Liberia.

"We cannot live for ourselves.

> A thousand fibers connect us with our fellow man; and
> along those fibers, as sympathetic threads, our actions run as
> causes, and they come back to us as effects." **—Melville**

Mentoring happens when we live for God.

Someone is always watching.

We do mentor unaware.

But sometimes we must also purpose to mentor, consciously guiding others into truth.

We are God's team.

Some of us are cheerleaders.

"You have heard me teach many things that have been confirmed by many reliable witnesses. Teach these great truths to trustworthy people who are able to pass them on to others." (Note 5)

Her name is Hope and she lives up to that name.

She came to a conference in 1990 where I was speaking on the topic, *"Women Under Construction."*

We got to meet personally that day and share lunch.

Hope wanted a legacy of faith in her life.

I challenged her to begin.

She did.

Through the years, her desire to grow with God has only increased.

Every time I have spoken in an area where she could attend, she has been there.

A love for her flowered so easily.

She encouraged me.

Hope was naturally a mentor.

Notes would come in the mail.

Precious, small but endearing gifts.

A conscious discipling began through prayer.

Prayer journals were kept when I would speak on mission to The British Isles.

Somebody is always praying us through.

My turn came to pray her through when she went to Chiang, Thailand.

Taking my tape sets of *"Becoming A Woman of Balance"* Hope wanted to encourage them, to leave something behind.

When my writing began, she would give away books as a way to mentor others.

Organizing women's events at her church and leading women's ministries were opportunities of growth assumed with a sense of challenge.

She counseled women who were struggling.

She was there when loss came.

They were there when it came to her.

Loss comes to each of us.

Always seeking and reaching, that's Hope.

We prayed for the conception of her daughter, Grace and she came full of Grace.

A second pregnancy was ectopic.

She almost lost her life.

The baby was miscarried.

Her faith was intact.

A year later a friend named Cora Runkle Blinsmon was putting together a devotional study entitled *"The Pursuit of a Heart of Wisdom."* In it she took the women through a walk of faith in Romans.

Day Six was entitled "Rejoicing in Hope while Suffering."

"…And we rejoice in the hope of the glory of God. Not only so, but we rejoice in our sufferings because we know suffering produces perseverance; perseverance, character; and character, hope. And hope does not disappoint us, because God has poured out His Love into our hearts by the Holy Spirit, whom He has given us." (Note 6)

On that day she wrote about Hope and the ectopic pregnancy.

"The baby was dearly wanted and longed for, much prayer blanketed them both. Still tragedy befell the family...I was sure of one powerful thing—that my friend's faith in God would not waver. I can barely describe what a tremendous, overwhelming feeling it was to see my friend walk in the deepest pit of pain with her arms outstretched above her head, seeking, reaching, calling and singing to the only One who could and would rescue her. My friend could rejoice, not because she was suffering but because her hope was in God. He did rescue her but not before many were touched. One day she asked me a question during a painful time, 'How are you suffering? Can you thank God for trusting you with this experience even if He never tells you why?'"

God is our hope.

And a woman named Hope gave it to her friend.

She also put her thoughts into a booklet to help other women cope through miscarriage, for loss must be recognized and worked through with God.

In time another baby girl named Faith joined her sister Grace.

What precious privilege she has.

Hope is enjoying guiding these little ones.

Mothering does not last forever.

Hope and her husband, Will, are a team that God put together.

They have learned to thank God through career changes, financial adjustment, the birth of children and loss.

She is also mentoring a college student at Duke, remembering how fragile life is at this time and how much a young person needs Godly friendship.

Thanking God for suffering does produce the ability to endure, and character does develop for hope is produced.

The scripture says, *"Hope does not disappoint us."*

My friend Hope has never disappointed me.

She continues to grow the harvest found in a satisfied life through Jesus Christ.

"Without faith it is impossible to please God for he who comes to God must believe that HE is, and that He is a rewarder." (Note 7)

God rewards with a harvest of faith because He is the reward.

"…I am your shield, your very great reward." (Note 8)

A purposeful journey leads us to Heaven.

It begins with mountains and valleys and the promise of rain.

God tells us He will care for this life by watching over it from the beginning of the year until the end.

He then gives us the requirement for blessing and the preparation for the harvest.

We are to obey, love and serve Him with all that we have.

If we do, He sends the spring rain and the autumn rain.

Our faith begins as a seed with the spring rain but the promise of autumn rain is more.

It is the faith with abundance.

A faith harvest.

We discover and embrace servanthood with joy because of purpose.

Our Father makes provision continually as we obey.

We live in satisfaction as we gather in abundance here and anticipate the glory of Heaven there.

What are you going to do with the rest of your life?

Are you laboring with expectation in the vineyard that is yours?

What on earth are we doing to prepare for Heaven?

Whom are we taking along with us?

Think, sing, meditate, write and act upon it every day.

Our whole life should be outreach.

Running toward God not running away.

We all run somewhere.

Jonah ran from God.

He did not want to go and do what God wanted.

"...Jonah ran away from the Lord." (Note 9)

And so do we.

Trying to escape responsibility, he boarded a ship bound for Tarshish.

Thought a trip might be the answer.

Trouble came.

A storm brewed.

Jonah was discovered to be the cause.

"I know it is my fault that this great storm has come upon you." (Note 10)

Disobedience breeds trouble.

God knows all.

He watches over His own.

A great fish was made ready to receive Jonah.

It just happened by when he was tossed overboard.

JAWS to the rescue!

Three miserable days later he called out to the God he knew for deliverance.

How long will it take us?

God heard.

He delivered Jonah.

Same message second time around.

He was to go to Ninevah, a wicked city that needed to be delivered from the ravages of sin.

God is the author of the second chance, the fat chance and the last chance.

He called to Jonah again.

This time Jonah heard.

Going in obedience to God, Jonah gave them truth and they repented.

Thousands were saved from utter destruction.

"The Ninevites believed God." (Note 11)

What a monumental victory.

Short lived in Jonah's mind.

The people deserved to die.

A loving God intervened.

He still does.

Sending folks like you and me to people who need a Savior.

They deserve to die;

So do we.

But a loving God continues to intervene.

Jonah could not enjoy the fruit of Godly labor.

A self-serving Jonah again retreated.

So can we.

What will we do?

Run toward God or run away from Him?

Words penned from an African native say it best.

I AM NOT ASHAMED

I am part of the fellowship of the unashamed.

The die is cast.

I have stepped over the line; the decision has been made;

I'm a disciple of His.

I won't look back, let up, slow down, back away or sit still.

My past is forgiven, my present makes sense and my future is secure.

I'm finished and done with low-living, sight-walking, small-planning, smooth knees, colorless dreams, tamed visions, mundane talking, chincy giving and puny goals.

I don't need prosperity, position, promotions, plaudits or popularity.

I don't have to be first, tops, recognized, praised, regarded or rewarded.

I now live by Grace, walk by Faith and labor by His Power.

My face is set.

My goal is heaven. My road is narrow.
My way is rough. My Guide is reliable, My mission is clear.

I cannot be bought, compromised, detoured,
lured away, turned back, deluded or delayed.
I will not flinch in the face of sacrifice, hesitate in the presence of the adversary,
negotiate at the table of the enemy nor ponder at the pool of popularity.

I won't give up, shut up, let up until I have stayed up, prayed up,
paid up for the cause of my Lord Jesus Christ.
I am a disciple of His.
I must go till He comes, give till I drop,
speak till all know and work till He stops me.
And when He comes for His own,
I don't want Him to have any trouble recognizing me.
I want my colors to be clear.

The first time I read this, I choked back tears, but I did not stop.
Each time I read it, my resolve becomes clearer.
My purpose grows. My faith flourishes.
I glimpse the glory of Heaven. I trust God.

He will send the autumn rain.
A faith harvest will come.
I'm hoping for a bumper crop.

"The people I have shaped for myself will broadcast my praise." (Note 12)

I have decided to be one of them.

Will you join me?

A PRAYER COVENANT

My Gracious God;

I am not ashamed of the Gospel.

I want my life to bloom with rich and recognizable faith

I want to serve YOU.

YOU don't need me but I need YOU.

I want to plant seeds of hope and love where lives have been ravaged.

I want fresh faith each day.

Storms will come to destroy what I have planted.

If they do, I will begin again.

The promise of Heaven is wooing me.

Stir me to take others with me.

Position Purpose every day in my thought life and grow it until I don't have to choose it for it will be rooted.

Nurture the indescribable joy I feel in Your Presence daily.

Strengthen me for I am weak.

When I am discouraged, stir that great crowd of witnesses to cheer me on

Grow more of YOU in me.

I choose to come, deny, take up my cross and follow YOU.

And when YOU come for me, know that I shall be looking lovingly for Your Face.

Lord, send the Autumn Rain.

About the Author

Billie Cash is an international retreat and conference speaker/musician. She has authored two other books, *Windows of Assurance* and *Light Breaking Through*. With humor and insight she brings accountability. A fresh authenticity in God's Word and personal application are the keys to her ministry.

Billie Cash
1605 N. Germantown Pkwy; Suite 111
Cordova, TN 38018

www.billiecash.com
or brcash@midsouth.rr.com

I would love to hear from you!

Index of Bible Translations

All scripture used is from the *New International Version* unless otherwise indicated.

Other translations used:

CEV *Contemporary English Version*
Grand Rapids: Zondervan (1965)

KJV *King James Version*
New York: American Bible Society (1611)

LB *Living Bible*
Wheaton: Tyndale House (1979)

Msg *The Message*
Colorado Springs: Navpress (1993)

NASB *New American Standard*
Anaheim: Foundation Press (1978)

NIV *New International Version*
Colorado Springs: International Bible Society (1978)

NJB *New Jerusalem Bible*
Garden City: Doubleday (1985)

NLB *New Living Translation*
Wheaton: Tyndale House (1996)

Notes

One

1. Romans 8:37
2. *Carmichael*: Amy Carmichael, *Edges of His Ways* (Fort Washington: Christian Literature Crusade, 1998), 146
3. Matthew 16:24a
4. Proverbs 28:26
5. Psalm 32:5
6. Acts 17:28
7. Isaiah 54:2
8. Hebrews 3:13

Two

1. Genesis 6:9
2. Genesis 6:11
3. Genesis 6:12b
4. Genesis 6:15
5. Genesis 7:5
6. Genesis 5:32
7. Acts 17:26b
8. II Chronicles 26:10
9. II Chronicles 26:7
10. II Chronicles 26:5
11. Proverbs 11:28 (Msg)

Three

1. *Eldredge*: John Eldredge, *Waking The Dead* (Nashville: Thomas Nelson, 2003), 105
2. Ibid
3. I Samuel 16:11
4. I Samuel 16:12
5. Psalm 86:11
6. II Samuel 11:1
7. II Samuel 11:9
8. II Samuel 11:27
9. II Samuel 12:7
10. II Samuel 12:13
11. *Morris*: Harold Morris, *The Law of the Harvest* (Nantucket: Wilson, 2000), 11
12. II Samuel 12:24b
13. Ezekiel 11:19a

Four

1. Psalm 16:8
2. *McManus*: Erwin Raphael McManus, *Seizing Your Divine Moment* (Nashville: Thomas Nelson 2002), 44
3. Deuteronomy 30:11-14
4. Psalm 55:1a

Five

1. *Yancy*: Philip Yancy edited by James Calvin Schaap, *More Than Words* (Grand Rapids: Baker 2002), 120-121
2. Romans 8:35
3. *Piper*: John Piper, *Don't Waste Your Life* (Wheaton: Crossway 2003), 33
4. *Baldacci*: David Baldacci, *The Christmas Train* (New York: Warner 2002), 52
5. I John 5:4
6. Hebrews 4:16
7. *Helms*: Hal M Helms, *Echoes of Eternity Volume II*. (Brewster: Paraclete Press 1998), 16

Six

1. Psalm 42:11
2. Proverbs 3:5
3. Ephesians 3:19
4. Ephesians 3:16
5. II Chronicles 16:9
6. *Mc Manus*: Erwin Raphael Mc Manus, *Seizing Your Divine Moment* (Nashville: Thomas Nelson 2002), 71
7. Ibid, 69

Seven

1. II Chronicles 5:13
2. *Jeremiah*: David Jeremiah, *A Bend in the Road* (Nashville: Word 2000), 50
3. II Kings 6:17a
4. *McManus*: Erwin Raphael Mc Manus, *Uprising* (Nashville: Thomas Nelson 2003), 127
5. *Piper*: John Piper, *Desiring God* (Sisters: Multnomah 1996), 100.
6. Jeremiah 9:24
7. *Starr*: Mirabai Starr, translator, St John of the Cross, *Dark Night of the Soul* (Riverhead: New York 2002), 148-149
8. Acts 17:27b
9. *Mc Manus*: Erwin Raphael, *Uprising* (Nashville: Thomas Nelson 2003), 89.
10. *Carmichael*: Amy Carmichael, *Gold by Moonlight* (London: Dohnavur 1943), 3
11. Ibid, 105
12. *Starr:* Mirabai Starr, translator, St. John of the Cross, *Dark Night of the Soul* (Riverhead: New York 2002), 15

Eight

1. Philippians 4:4-7
2. I Thessalonians 5:18
3. I Thessalonians 3:12
4. Colossians 1:16 (Msg)
5. Romans 1:1a
6. Romans 1:14-15
7. Acts 9:4-5
8. Acts 9:9
9. Acts 9:15a
10. *Vance*: James I. Vance, D. D., L.L.D. *The Life of Service* (New York: Fleming H. Revell 1918), 111
11. John 4:9b
12. John 4:14
13. John 4:39- 41
14. Hebrews 6:7
15. Psalm 138:8a

Nine

1. Romans 7:15
2. II Timothy 2:13 (LB)
3. Colossians 1:27
4. Acts 7:9b-10

5. John 21:17

6. *Cymbala*: Jim Cymbala, *The Life God Blesses* (Grand Rapids: Zondervan 2001), 74

Ten

1. Ezekiel 34:26-27
2. *Chapman*: Marie Manire Chapman article *"It May Be Today"* Composer's Favorite (New York: Christian Missionary Alliance Periodical 1975), 16
3. *Coleman*; Nancy Coleman, article *"For Her, Life is a Symphony"* (Waverly: The Review newspaper 1997), 1c
4. Isaiah 61:3 (LB)
5. *Warren*: Rick Warren, *The Purpose Driven Life* (Grand Rapids: Zondervan 2002), 64
6. Psalm 98:4
7. Isaiah 46:4 (Msg)
8. Psalm 98:1
9. Judges 5:3b
10. Romans 6:13 (NLT)

Eleven

1. Colossians 2:7 (NLT)
2. *Cash:* Johnny Cash with Patrick Carr *Cash, The Autobiography of Johnny Cash* (San Francisco: Harper 1997), 225
3. Ibid, 201-202
4. John 8:31 (NASB, 1978 edition)
5. Philippians 1:6 (LB)
6. Matthew 9:11 (KJV)
7. I Corinthians 9:22b
8. *Cash*: Johnny Cash with Patrick Carr, *Cash: The Autobiography of Johnny Cash* (San Francisco: Harper 1997), 222
9. *Eichenberg:* Fritz Eichenberg,

illustrator, edited by The Bruderhof, *The Gospel in Dostoyevsky*, foreword by Malcolm Muggeridge, (Farmington: Plough 1998), 3

Twelve

1. Philippians 4:4-5
2. Psalm 24:1a
3. Acts 13:36
4. Proverbs 19:21
5. II Corinthians 12:10 (NIV)
6. Hebrews 4:15 (CEV)
7. Romans 8:26a
8. *Colson:* Chuck Colson, *The Body* (Dallas: Word 1992), 329
9. Colson: Chuck Colson, quoted on Breakpoint, Prison Fellowship web site, 2004, p.1
10. *Hybels:* Bill Hybels, *Descending Into Greatness* (Grand Rapids: Zondervan 1993), 154
11. Ibid
12. John 15:5b

Thirteen

1. Psalm 133:2b
2. Psalm 103:4-5
3. Philippians 4:11-13
4. Jeremiah 17:7-8 (NLT)
5. II Timothy: 2:2 (NLT)
6. Romans 5:3-5
7. Hebrews 11:6
8. Genesis 15:1b
9. Jonah 1:3a
10. Jonah 1:12b
11. Jonah 3:5
12. Isaiah 43:21 (NJB)

WINDOWS OF ASSURANCE

In her Journey of Prayer, Billie Cash shares the resources she used to persevere as a school girl in 33 different schools. Those experiences propelled Billie into the artificial light of the theater; but it was the penetrating light of God's presence that birthed identity and ready resolve. For each window she opened, His love met her with grace and called her to test the real release of prevailing prayer.

ISBN: 1 889893 59 5
$12.99/£8.99 (224 pp)

LIGHT BREAKING THROUGH

Light. The visible reminder of Invisible Light. (T. S. Eliot) The light of God searches all things, our struggles, lonliness and brokenness. This book lets us experience that light, as it breaks through our struggles, intercepting us with truth, love, and fresh insights at every turn, in every season. He urges us onward, to continue, to grow, to believe, to love, and to finish our race, giving us illumination in the darkest days. We can trust His Light.

ISBN: 1 889893 97 8
$9.99/£6.99 (144 pp)